"This book concerns a fundamental top. Self. The authors bring an incredible range and depth of expertise to it. Spagnolo is a psychoanalyst and paediatric neurologist; Northoff is a neuroscientist, psychiatrist and philosopher. The result is an intellectual banquet of clinical descriptions, science and philosophy, with extremely rich theorizing."

Mark Solms, Research Chair of the International Psychoanalytical Association; Co-Chair of the International Neuropsychoanalysis Society

"The case of psychoanalysis remains a puzzle. You can look at it as a form of treatment, or as a scientific approach to the study of the mind, or as a philosophical topic. But you always find the same mixed response: on the one hand, you encounter great success, a large following, and a multitude of sensation seekers; on the other hand, you find the critics and the controversy.

The death of psychoanalysis has been announced and postponed but it never took place. Ironically, in spite of no death, there already is a revival of psychoanalysis. The branch of it that carries the day concerns the natural marriage of psychoanalysis and neuroscience which began with the work of Mark Solms and has only gained in strength. To this setting come Rosa Spagnolo and Georg Northoff with a welcome addition to the pertinent literature. They aim at explaining each side of the partnership to the other side and their effort will reward the intellectually curious and the practical minded alike. I wish them great success."

Antonio Damasio, author, The Strange Order of Things; Dornsife Professor of Neuroscience, Psychology & Philosophy; Director, Brain and Creativity Institute, University of Southern California, Los Angeles, USA

"Is it possible to build a bridge between two different, but intertwined, disciplines such as psychoanalysis and neuroscience? What is the glue that aligns together the different elements of this bridge? For Rosa Spagnolo and Georg Northoff, the Self, and its dynamic at psychological and neuronal level, might be the candidate.

Several psychoanalysts like Jung, Kohut, Winnicott, Modell, Bromberg, and neuroscientists like Northoff, Panksepp, Damasio, Solms and Schore, just to name a few, tried to define the intrinsic sense of subjectivity that characterize our psyche. The Self is shaped by the alignment with the world where the intra/inter-psychic structure is nurtured by a good enough interaction with the animate environment.

In this book, departing from the building blocks represented by time and space, moving through the relation with the body, the other, the world and finally to the dreams, the Self is disentangled in its own dynamic features.

The continuous integration of the spatio-temporal approach with psycho-dynamic processes behind the transformation of the Self is highly innovative and sheds a novel perspective on the case histories reported.

Wisely describing clinical experiences, *The Dynamic Self* aims at looking for the continuity in the relation between psychoanalysis and neuroscience, emphasizing how they might be two sides of a coin informing psychotherapy and psychoanalytic treatment. The spatio-temporal approach will have huge implications for psychotherapy and future research."

Andrea Scalabrini, PhD, PsyD; Neuroscientist and Psychotherapist-Psychoanalyst; Post-doc researcher at University G. d'Annunzio of Chieti-Pescara, Italy

The Dynamic Self in Psychoanalysis

The Dynamic Self in Psychoanalysis builds a bridge between two different but intertwined disciplines—psychoanalysis and neuroscience—by examining the Self and its dynamics at the psychological and neuronal level.

Rosa Spagnolo and Georg Northoff seek continuity in the relationship between psychoanalysis and neuroscience, emphasizing how both inform psychotherapy and psychoanalytic treatment and exploring the transformations of the Self that occur during this work. Each chapter presents clinical examples which demonstrate the evolution of the spatiotemporal and affective dimensions of the Self in a variety of psychopathologies. Spagnolo and Northoff analyze the possible use of new neuroscientific findings to improve clinical treatment in psychodynamic therapy and present a spatio-temporal approach that has significant implications for the practice of psychotherapy and for future research.

The Dynamic Self in Psychoanalysis will be of great interest to psychoanalysts, psychotherapists, neuroscientists and neuropsychiatrists.

Rosa Spagnolo, MD, is a child neuropsychiatrist, child and adolescent psychotherapist and psychoanalyst based in Italy. She is a member of the Italian Psychoanalytical Society (SPI), the IPA and the NPSA, and co-founder of the Italian Psychoanalytic Dialogues Association. She is the editor of *Building Bridges: The Impact of Neuropsychoanalysis on Psychoanalytic Clinical Sessions* (Routledge).

Georg Northoff, MD, PhD, FRCP, is a neuroscientist, philosopher, and psychiatrist. He is one of the world's leading scientists in the field of brain and mind, having established neurophilosophy and, more recently, a novel approach to brain–mind relationship in terms of time–space dynamic. He is the author of *Neuropsychoanalysis in Practice* (Oxford, 2011) and *Neurophilosophy and the Healthy Mind* (Norton, 2016), as well as a Professor at the University of Ottawa in Canada and holds multiple affiliations to universities in Europe and Asia.

The Dynamic Self in Psychoanalysis

Neuroscientific Foundations and Clinical Cases

Rosa Spagnolo and Georg Northoff

Routledge
Taylor & Francis Group

LONDON AND NEW YORK

First published 2022
by Routledge
2 Park Square, Milton Park, Abingdon, Oxon OX14 4RN

and by Routledge
605 Third Avenue, New York, NY 10158

Routledge is an imprint of the Taylor & Francis Group, an informa business

British Library Cataloguing-in-Publication Data
A catalogue record for this book is available from the British Library

Library of Congress Cataloging-in-Publication Data
A catalog record has been requested for this book

ISBN: 978-1-032-11439-2 (hbk)
ISBN: 978-0-367-42896-9 (pbk)
ISBN: 978-1-003-22187-6 (ebk)

DOI: 10.4324/9781003221876

Typeset in Times New Roman
by Taylor & Francis Books

Contents

Preface

The study of the mind from a psychoanalytic perspective, and the brain in neuroscience, cannot take place without the mutual and dynamic relation between the Self and the other/world.

Learning the lesson from infant research, development psychology, and neuroscience, together with clinical and psychodynamic psychotherapeutic practice, only the continuous dialectical exchange between the Self and the other/world creates the basis for continuity, integration, and, as I would like to emphasize, creativity.

This is what happens here in this brilliant and outstanding work written by Rosa Spagnolo and Georg Northoff, a creative and dynamic relation between psychoanalysis and neuroscience that has its roots in philosophical, physical, medical, and humanistic disciplines.

The studies on Self, identity, psychopathology, and the conscious–unconscious dynamics of both authors are here intertwined in a creative and fine-grained understanding of the mind, the brain, and especially the therapeutic process. Moreover, the richness of the interdisciplinary perspectives and reflections on the 'Dynamics of Self' sinks into a profound philosophical and existential vision that is never reductionist nor simplistic or scientist.

Freud himself tried in his early writing *Project for a scientific psychology* (Freud, 1895) to connect psychoanalysis and neuroscience, but later he focused only on psychoanalysis, and gave up his ambitious project. Timing was not there for Freud, neither for Jung, that in his writing *The undiscovered self* (1957) wrote: 'The structure and physiology of the brain furnish no explanation of the psychic process' (Jung, 1976, p. 33). Luckily nowadays, there is a renewed interest in developing a new project for a scientific psychology (Solms, 2020).

However, in another writing Jung proposed to consider the brain as: 'A transformer station, in which the relatively infinite tension or intensity of the psyche proper is transformed into perceptible frequencies or "extensions"' (Jung, 1976, p. 43–47).

At that time there were not many chances to study the brain's dynamics, but Jung still envisioned how the brain/mind might be conceived in a spatio-temporal dimension working through its own frequencies or 'extensions', i.e. what here are called 'Dynamics of the Self'.

The relation between the Self and the world through time and space is here proposed as essential for the definition of the Self, as an inter-dependent entity characterized by its extended duration in time from past to future passing through the present. In its own continuity–discontinuity, unity–multiplicity, the Self represents the subjective glue that informs our existence and its underlying dynamics (Scalabrini et al., 2020a; Scalabrini et al., 2021).

What are the dynamics behind the complexity of the Self? Is the Self unitary or multiple? How can we experience Self-continuity? These are just some of the questions the authors try to clarify over the chapters while working through contemporary case histories.

The single cases represent the animate and relational *'online'* laboratory where the authors test:

—the influence of Psychoanalysis (Wallerstein, 2002);
—the inclusion of affective neuroscience in psychoanalytic treatment (Spagnolo, 2018; Mucci, 2018); and, going one step further,
—a spatio-temporal approach (Northoff, 2013; Northoff et al., 2019, 2020).

Leaving aside the generalizability of the results, here single cases represent the extreme value of subjectivity and their profound human nature. The studies of human beings, the two subjectivities involved in therapy with their own background and biography, working through ruptures and repairs, affect sharing and regulation, enactment, and all the different features of what concerns the complex relational matrix where they are deeply involved, is the biggest contribution of this book.

Leaving from the basement of space and time, *The Dynamic Self* reveals configurations in the relationships between the body, other, world, creativity–madness, and dreams through each different clinical case. Every case marks different self-knots that manifest different aspects of the Self and the specific role of psychotherapy. Each vignette is the story of a Self that could not take place in time and in space to different degrees. Traumatic experiences, compensatory strategies together with defence mechanisms did not allow the Self to be part of the world, leaving traces in the spontaneous activity of the brain.

Nowadays, different from the Freudian conception of trauma and repression, it is clear how traumatic experiences together with dissociative processes leave traces in the Self and ultimately in the brain itself (Mucci, 2021). From a neuropsychodynamic vantage point Allan Schore (2003) and Clara Mucci (2018) show how trauma strongly impacts Self and brain development. The relational trauma (that needs to be distinguished from the trauma of natural catastrophes) might be conceived as a continuum of severity and depth moving from:

—first level of trauma, i.e. early relational misattunement between caregiver and child during first years of life;

—second level of trauma, i.e. trauma of human agency due to severe deprivation, neglect, abuse (Mucci, 2013);

—third level of trauma, i.e. massive social trauma and intergenerational transmission.

The effect of traumatic experience might result in dissociation at different levels (Scalabrini et al., 2020b; Mucci & Scalabrini, 2021).

In this regard our restless brain is characterized by its own spontaneous activity and its spatio-temporal structure that contains the information related to the Self and its conscious–unconscious–processual memory. Thus, when the basis of our Self in its underlying world–brain relation is disrupted or even lost, non-integration of internal and external stimuli might occur, leading to alterations in embodiment and, even further, the disruption of our Self's relationship with the world and its continuity. This failure can thus be seen as a disconnection that threatens both the sense of subjectivity and intersubjectivity, leading to different forms of psychopathology.

Here psychoanalysis together with neuroscience takes the role of the transformation function where the two brains (in accordance with Jung vision) work as 'transformer stations' where the tension of the two psyches is transformed into frequencies and dynamics. This process is here seen as a vehicle to re-establish the necessary alignment for the continuity and the expansion of the Self from private, to public, to world (Scalabrini et al., 2018).

The spatio-temporal approach represents a novel point of view on psychic processes and psychopathology. Importantly this approach does not exclude the others and seems to be coherent with what is the target of investigation for contemporary relational psychoanalysis and neuropsychoanalysis emphasizing the role of affective neuroscience, personality, and Self-development together with psychopathology (Bromberg, 2011; Cozolino, 2017; Mucci 2018; Panksepp, 1998; Panksepp and Biven, 2012; Schore, 1994, 2003; Siegel, 2020; Solms, 2018, 2020). Simply put, the spatiotemporal approach targets a deeper layer, that is the brain's spatial and temporal features constituting the dynamic and topographical organization of the Self, which in turn shapes and contains affective, social, and cognitive functions. The spatio-temporal approach thus aims to embed and integrate the different aspects of the psyche, providing a more comprehensive, basic, and extensive operating field.

How does this spatio-temporal approach also embed psychotherapy? What is the main aim of the psychotherapeutic process according to this approach?

Here it is proposed that psychotherapy unfolds in a shared time and space between the therapist and the patient allowing the patient's Self to experience what was lost or was not allowed in order to be part of the time of the world. This work represents a shift aiming to integrate psychodynamic and psychoanalytic principles with a novel configuration named temporospatial psychotherapy. This conception proposes to consider the very fundamental basis of our brain and mind. Time and space not only represent the building blocks of our novel neuroscientific understanding of the brain, but also find their common and respective features in mind and in their phenomenological manifestations. The world and its narratives, together with transference–countertransference dynamics, unfold in time and space, and the same is true for the Self that is part of the world.

Spatiotemporal psychotherapy is here proposed as a chance to re-establish the subjective sense of time and space of Self that is nested in its own relationship with body, other and finally the world. This process might be seen as a basic process representing a target of psychotherapy that aims to constitute a dynamic re-organization of the brain and the Self.

Here, spatio-temporal psychotherapy is considered the main road to understand and heal the Self and its conscious–unconscious processes through synchronous alignment.

Now, finally, the Self can be 'brought back into the world'!

Andrea Scalabrini, Phd, PsyD
Neuroscientist and Psychotherapist-Psychoanalyst
Affiliated Analytical Psychologist at CIPA (Centro Italiano di Psicologia Analitica) and IAAP (International Association for Analytical Psychology)
Post-doc researcher at University G. d'Annunzio of Chieti-Pescara, Italy

References

Bromberg, M. P. (2011). *The Shadow of the Tsunami: and the Growth of the Relational Mind*. London/New York: Routledge.

Cozolino, L. (2017). *The neuroscience of psychotherapy: healing the social brain (Norton Series on Interpersonal Neurobiology)*. New York: W W Norton & Company.

Freud, S. (1895). *Project for a scientific psychology*. S.E., 1:281–391. London: Hogarth.

Jung, C.G. (1976). *Letters Vol. II* (1951–1961) (pp. 43–47). London/New York: Routledge.

Jung, C. G. (2014). The Undiscovered Self. In *Collected Works of CG Jung, Vol.10*. Princeton: Princeton University Press.

Mucci, C. (2013). *Beyond individual and collective trauma: Intergenerational transmission, psychoanalytic treatment, and the dynamics of forgiveness*. London/New York: Routledge.

Mucci, C. (2018). *Borderline Bodies: Affect Regulation Therapy for Personality Disorders (Norton Series on Interpersonal Neurobiology)*. New York: WW Norton & Company.

Mucci, C. (2021). Dissociation vs repression: A new neuropsychoanalytic model for psychopathology. *The American Journal of Psychoanalysis*:1–30. https://doi.org/10.1057/s11231-021-09279.

Mucci, C. & Scalabrini, A. (2021). Traumatic effects beyond diagnosis: The impact of dissociation on the mind-body-brain system. *Psychoanalytic Psychology*, in press.

Northoff, G. (2013). What the brain's intrinsic activity can tell us about consciousness? A tri-dimensional view. *Neuroscience & Biobehavioral Reviews*, 37(4):726–738.

Northoff, G., Wainio-Theberge, S., & Evers, K. (2019). Is temporo-spatial dynamics the 'common currency' of brain and mind? *Physics of Life Reviews*, 33:34–54.

Northoff, G., Wainio-Theberge, S., & Evers, K. (2020). Spatiotemporal neuroscience–what is it and why we need it. *Physics of Life Reviews*, 33:78–87.

Panksepp, J. (1998). *Affective neuroscience: The foundations of human and animal emotions*. Oxford: Oxford University Press.

Panksepp, J., & Biven, L. (2012). *The archaeology of mind: neuroevolutionary origins of human emotions*. New York: WW Norton & Company.

Scalabrini, A., Mucci, C., & Northoff, G. (2018). Is our self related to personality? A neuropsychodynamic model. *Frontiers in human neuroscience*, 12(346):1–9.

Scalabrini, A., Mucci, C., Angeletti, L. L., & Northoff, G. (2020a). The self and its world: a neuro-ecological and temporo-spatial account of existential fear. *Clinical Neuropsychiatry*, 17(2): 46–58.

Scalabrini, A., Mucci, C., Esposito, R., Damiani, S., & Northoff, G. (2020b). Dissociation as a disorder of integration–On the footsteps of Pierre Janet. *Progress in Neuro-Psychopharmacology and Biological Psychiatry*, 101:109928. doi:10.1016/j.pnpbp.2020.109928.

Scalabrini, A., Xu, J., & Northoff, G. (2021). What COVID-19 tells us about the self–the deep inter-subjective and cultural layers of our brain. *Psychiatry and clinical neurosciences*, 75(2):37–45.

Schore, A. N. (1994). *Affect regulation and the origin of the self: The neurobiology of emotional development*. London/New York: Routledge.

Schore, A. N. (2003). *Affect dysregulation and disorders of the self (Norton Series on interpersonal neurobiology)*. New York: W W Norton & Company.

Siegel, D. J. (2020). *The developing mind: How relationships and the brain interact to shape who we are*. New York: Guilford Publications.

Solms, M. (2018). *The feeling brain: Selected papers on neuropsychoanalysis*. London/New York: Routledge.

Solms, M. (2020). New project for a scientific psychology: General scheme. *Neuropsychoanalysis*, 22(1–2), 5–35.

Spagnolo, R. (2018). *Building Bridges: The Impact of Neuropsychoanalysis on Psychoanalytic Clinical Sessions*. London/New York: Routledge.

Wallerstein, R. S. (2002). Psychoanalytic treatments within psychiatry: an expanded view. *Archives of general psychiatry*, 59(6): 499–500.

Introducing the Dynamic Self

Dynamic Self—Spatiotemporal structure in brain and psyche

Since its inception, psychoanalysis has focused on the mutual influence between the world and the environment, on the one hand, and the mind and brain, on the other, seeking this influence in the patients' clinical and biographical stories. Freud's early works show some of these crossroads between nature and culture, where the neurotic symptom takes shape (Freud, 1894a), marked by the conflicting relationship between the intrapsychic instances: Ego, Id, Super Ego. Only after becoming well established in the scientific community of the time, psychoanalysis broadened its horizon to include relations with external objects. This new attention to the quality of the object relationship led to the concept of the Self within the psychoanalytic movement. From Winnicott, Fairbairn, and Kohut onwards, this focus has never been abandoned, and it has become enriched with new insights from closely related fields such as neuropsychology, philosophy, and neuroscience.

Our emphasis on the transformations of the Self, referred to as 'the Dynamic Self', combines the focus on current changes for individuals and communities, with the scientific contributions of neuroscience to psychoanalysis. The presentation of the clinical cases in psychoanalytic treatment can become a guide to trace the intersections between psychoanalytic and neuropsychodynamic models. The starting point is the description of the spatiotemporal structure of the Self (Northoff, 2016; Northoff, 2017; Huang et al., 2016; Wolff et al., 2019), the use and evolution of defence mechanisms and the transformations of the Self occurring throughout the psychoanalytic treatment.

We hereby propose some brief considerations, keeping the focus on the dialogue between psychoanalysis and neuroscience (Spagnolo, 2018; Boeker et al., 2018). Like a path winding from the bodily Self through embodiment and disembodiment up to its representations into the dream, the book provides various descriptions of the Self and its complexity.

The Self can be understood as a mnemonic laboratory with different time dimensions, like past–present–future (Edelman, 1989), shaped, and informed, by coexisting childhood and adult life (Stern, 1985; Tronick, 2007). From this

DOI: 10.4324/9781003221876-1

time perspective, the Self can be conceived as featuring an 'extended duration' over time: it makes the past endure in the present, which, in turn, affects the future. In our case studies, such 'extended duration' connects neuroscientific data with psychodynamic features of the Self.

The extended duration allows the Self to integrate different time scales related to different motor, cognitive, affective, sensory functions (Palombo, 2018). These functions are held together by this 'subjective glue', the temporal glue of the extended duration of the Self that continuously builds its inner time (and space) structure. It is a multi-layered structure, with different configurations which appear to be more cohesive or disintegrated, depending on the defence mechanisms. Its subjective space–time structure (Northoff, 2016; Northoff, 2017; Wolff et al., 2019) shapes our being in the world and finds its unitary vision both in its bodily and narrative dimensions.

Most interestingly, the recent data show that the spatiotemporal structure of the Self can ultimately be traced to, and is based on, the brain's spatiotemporal structure, especially the one along the midline of the cerebral cortex, called Cortical Midline Structures (CMS). Thanks to their broad connections to other regions in the brain, they can have an impact on all the other functions through their subjective space and time dimension. In this way, the Self temporalizes and spatializes the brain, and its associated psychological functions, in a subjective way. Therefore, there is a basic subjectivity of the spatiotemporal structure of the Self in the neuronal activity of the brain as well as in its various psychological functions. This basic subjectivity, and its brain and psyche manifestations, including its alterations, are the main topic of the present book.

Facets of the Self: I—The Self in psychoanalysis

Psychoanalytic theory provided a major contribution to the development of the concept of the Self. Today, it is still possible to capitalize on these models in psychodynamic therapy. In the years 1930–1950, the Self was introduced into the psychoanalytic community as a set of split elements, projectively dislocated in the environment and re-introduced as inner objects (Klein et al., 1952; Winnicott, 1965; Fairbairn & Scharff, 1988/1994; Kohut, 1971; Kohut, 1977). It was then understood as a single element extended outwards to include the environment or as a multiple and fragmented entity (Bromberg, 1994; Bromberg, 2011; Lester, 2012). The interweaving of these latter features was well described in 2005 by Mills, in his critical article on the new trends in psychoanalysis that aimed at eclipsing the drive model in favour of the inter-subjective and relational model:

> Whereas some relational analysts advocate for a singular, cohesive self that is subject to change yet endures over time (Fosshage, 2003; Lichtenberg et al., 2002), others prefer to characterize selfhood as existing in multiplicity: rather than one self, there are 'multiple selves' (Bromberg, 1994; Mitchell, 1993).

But how is that possible? Envisioning multiple 'selves' is philosophically problematic on ontological grounds; it introduces a plurality of contradictory essences, obfuscates the nature of agency, and undermines the notion of freedom. Here we have the exact opposite position of indistinguishability: multiple selves are posited to exist as separate, distinct entities that presumably have the capacity to interact and communicate with one another and the analyst. But committing to a self-multiplicity thesis, rather than to a psychic monism that allows for differentiated and modified self-states, introduces the enigma of how competing existent entities would be able to interact, given that they would have distinct essences, which would prevent them from being able to intermingle to begin with.

(Mills, 2005, p. 170)

This psychoanalytic vision of the concrete nature of the Self, represented in, or through, its internal/external objects, was pitted against Lifton's (1993) extreme philosophical vision of a fluid and boundless Self, and Metzinger's (2003) of the Self without reality and consistency; like a deceptive internal operative model that has raised many perplexities in the field of the philosophy of the mind. Moreover, besides the representation of the internal objects in the Self, neurobiology, and the environment, have found a psychoanalytic echo in the words of Modell (1996):

The necessity to consider both biologic and social determinants concurrently can be readily illustrated when one turns to the concept of the self. For one cannot think of the self without simultaneously considering biological, personal, social and cultural dimensions.

(Modell, 1996, p. 5)

These points were expanded by Mitchell (1988, 2000), even if through different models. Mitchell managed to give greater consistency to the relational dimension introduced by clinical studies and by the concept of the Self as: 'An alternative perspective which considers the relations with others, not the drives, as the basic stuff of mental life' (Mitchell, 1988, p. 2).

In addition, we have:

—Sullivan's detailed interviews on the here and now of the analytical relationship (Mitchell, 1995);
—the internal operational models of Bowlby (1969);
—the mother–infant—infant–research regulatory exchanges by D. Stern (1985) and Beebe & Lachmann (1998, 2003);
—the organization of the presymbolic procedural codes (Beebe et al., 1997);
—the budding intersubjective psychoanalysis (Stolorow & Atwood, 1992).

All these authors found ample space in Mitchell's thought.

In fact, together with Greenberg (Greenberg & Mitchell, 1983), he proposed to overcome the Freudian model of the tripartite mind, that is the three instances—Ego, Id, Super Ego—with their conflicts for the primacy of the drives, and to abandon the concept of the mind individually constructed as a single unit, in favour of a model centred on the exchange between the Self and the Other.

Over the years, Mitchell (2000) described these Self–Other configurations along the lines of the me–you patterns and self–other configurations by Sullivan and Kernberg (1976), and of the relational matrix in which this configurations develop even through conscious–unconscious aggregations and disintegrations. These indeed paved the way to new psychoanalytic techniques, but, at the same time, stirred some controversy, as summarized by Mills (2005):

> Further statements such as 'There is *no* experience that is not interpersonally mediated' (Mitchell, 1992, p. 2, italics added) lend themselves to the social-linguistic platform and thereby deplete the notion of individuation, autonomy, choice, freedom, and teleological (purposeful) action, because we are constituted, and hence caused, by extrinsic forces that determine who we are. Not only does this displace the centrality of subjectivity- the very thing relationality wants to account for- it does not take into account other non-linguistic or extra-linguistic factors that transpire within personal lived experience, such as the phenomenology of embodiment, somatic resonance states, non-conceptual perceptive consciousness, affective life, aesthetic experience, a priori mental processes organized prior to the formal acquisition of language, and most important, the unconscious.
>
> (Mills, 2005, p. 170)

All these factors, just mentioned by Mills, are now widely considered in psychoanalysis; it will suffice to think of the production by Fonagy (Fonagy et al., 2004), and Schore (2003a, 2003b), for the developmental psychology and attachment theory, or the advances of contemporary American psychoanalysis (Cooper, 2006), in which the development of the Self closely follows the emotional and/or affective regulation. In this century, psychoanalysis, like philosophy, has also been enriched by the new knowledge and the new language coming from neuroscience, which is now the focus of our attention.

Facets of the Self: II—The Self in neuroscience and philosophy

Neuroscientific investigation has greatly emphasized the somatic origin of the Self, through the term embodiment, for example. Here, we consider the theories according to which 'embodied' is not only a factor to be added to cognition/memory to justify the link between mind and body; embodiment is a broader concept suggesting that the brain is not only the area where cognitive processes take place (Wilson & Golonka, 2013). These integrated body-mind processes also take shape through the development of the Self, as described by Tsakiris:

> The experience of body-ownership may represent a critical component of self-specificity as evidenced by the different ways in which multisensory integration that interacts with the inner models of the body can actually manipulate important physical and psychological aspects of the Self, thus inducing changes both in the body and in the mind.
>
> (Tsakiris, 2010, p. 22)

Through its somatic (biological) root, the Self responds to the homeostatic needs of metabolism (Damasio, 2010) and follows the alternation of life seasons from the beginnings of the first representations to the most complex configurations of adult life (Damasio, 2018). In addition to making emotions and feelings speak through their rootedness in the body, Damasio gives voice to the subjectivation of consciousness through the development of the Self. In *The feeling of what happens* (Damasio, 1999), consciousness is described as the 'knowledge of feeling', it is not perceived as an image, or as a visual, or auditory configuration, but it is a configuration constructed with the non-verbal signs of the states of the body.

Linking consciousness closely to the Self, Damasio identifies three levels of consciousness: the proto-Self, the nuclear Self, and the autobiographical Self. While the proto-Self is a still unaware state of consciousness, the nuclear Self is the first level of aware consciousness and coincides with the knowledge of feeling that emotion. The biological essence of the nuclear Self is the representation of a map of the proto-Self that is modified by interacting with the object, while the autobiographical Self, or extended consciousness, coincides with the higher level of consciousness. The autobiographical Self is based on the person's ability to keep track of his or her own story. The autobiographical Self is based on autobiographical memory, which is made up of implicit memories of many individual experiences of the past and of the expected/imagined future.

Panksepp too, like Damasio, describes the dimension of the development of the Self, nested on the primordial up to the metacognitive level (Panksepp & Biven, 2012). According to him, the body map is a proto-Self that, through the emergence of emotions and motivations in the primary process, evolves into the nuclear Self and, as better explained some years later:

> In spite of the fact that this structure has been called the 'core-Self' by a member of this research group (Panksepp, 1998b) and 'proto-Self' by Damasio (1999), here we prefer to adopt the definition of 'affective core-Self', in order to underline the absolute relevance of the affective dimension.
>
> (Alcaro et al., 2017, p. 4)

Panksepp adds the universal 'nomothetic' brain function to the term 'core Self': a trans-species concept of the Self which can be described by self-related processing (SRP) as a specific mode of interaction between organisms and the environment (Panksepp & Northoff, 2009). While processing raw feelings, the 'core Self' interacts with tertiary cognitive processes and promotes the emergence of 'idiographic', 'extended' unique Self.

> These primary to tertiary gradients of mental development ultimately yield nested-hierarchies of Brain Mind relationships [...] where the lower functions are re-represented within higher functions, providing multiple avenues of bottom-up and top-down relations—circular/two-way causal loops—that work as a coherent unit.
>
> (Panksepp et al., 2012, p. 10)

The emphasis on bodily and affective features of the Self implies that there is a dimension or layer in our Self that occurs prior to, and independent of, reflection and cognition; this has been described as core pre-reflective, and non-narrative aspects of the Self, called the Minimal Self (Zahavi, 2006; Hohwy, 2007), which has been a topic especially in the phenomenology and philosophy of the mind. Quoting Gallagher (2000):

> Ever since William James categorized different senses of the self at the end of the 19th century, philosophers and psychologists have refined and expanded the possible variations of this concept. James' inventory of physical self, mental self, spiritual self, and the ego has been variously supplemented.
>
> (Gallagher, 2000, p. 14)

According to him, the phenomenology of the Self allows us to approach two aspects of the Minimal Self: Self-ownership and Self-agency. The sense of ownership and the sense of agency are normally perceived as joint, but in some psychopathological cases, they can travel separately, thus enabling us to appreciate their individual peculiarities. The theorization of a Minimal Self has opened the door to a wide debate on the relationship between embodiment/disembodiment and first-person experience, for example, 'non-conceptual first-person content' (Gallagher, 2000). These thoughts revolve around the following topics:

—the ecological Self of Neisser (1967);
—the proposal by Strawson (1997) about the Self as a single mental entity, a subject aware of a local and momentary experience, not necessarily embedded in the environment;
—Metzinger's thought (2003) about 'no such thing as the Self exists';
—Noë (2004) and his concept of extended mind.

Facets of the Self: III—Pre-reflective Self and narrative Self

Let us dwell for a few more moments on the Minimal Self that, together with neuroscience and cognitive science, refers to the nuclear, primitive, aspects of the Self that make it possible to draw the boundaries with respect to the environment. In this field, the concept of the Self is sometimes accompanied by the concept of pre-reflective Self-consciousness that contains two main terms, 'pre-reflective' and 'Self-consciousness'. 'Pre-reflective' means that the experience of the Self does not stem from any reflection or cognitive operation and that it is simultaneously an inherent part of our experience and thus of our consciousness. Consequently, the Self is no longer outside of our consciousness, but it is an integral part of it, hence the second term, 'Self-consciousness'. Since the pre-reflectively experienced Self is the basis of all phenomenal features of our experience, it must be considered as essential for any subsequent cognitive activity (Northoff, 2018).

For example, Hohwy (2007) highlights three core cognitive tasks of the Self: Self in agency and bodily movement, Self in perception, Self in planning and attention, which, if missing, may be a serious impairment for the development of the Self.

> The conclusion is that core properties of the sense of Self are underpinned by properties of a unified fundamental cognitive brain system. This approach to the nature of the Self reveals the sense of minimal self as a sense of already being familiar with new sensory input, which is sustained by predicting what happens and, for the narrative self, of a see-saw between pondering one's role in a given task and forgetting oneself in the task. The self in agency and perception transpires as a predicting and pondering self.
>
> (Hohwy, 2007, p. 2)

In his last book, J. Palombo (2018) too describes how some recurrent developmental cognitive disorders have a strong impact on Self-development, thus emphasizing the importance of the cognitive skills of the Self. However, Hohwy makes a distinction between the autobiographical and narrative competences of the Self and the Minimal Self:

> As I indicated above, this experience of the minimal Self in perception is explained by properties associated with generative models and predictive coding. A feeling of mineness requires some kind of cognitive frame of reference in which to place the experience. This frame of reference cannot however be an autobiographical narrative, which is meant to be distinct from the minimal self.
>
> (Hohwy, 2007, p. 8)

Maraffa and Paternoster (2016) criticize both the assumption of a minimal form of the Self and reductionism, which leads to considering the non-existence of the Self. They write:

> In eliminative versions of narrativism, made popular mainly by Dennett (1991, 2005; see also Metzinger, 2003), the self simply does not exist: there is nothing but a confabulatory narrative elaborated by our brains to make sense of the chaotic flow of experience and make social relations more effective. We are proposing a naturalistic form of narrativism that radically dissents from any attempt to eliminate the self. Constructing and protecting an identity that is 'valid' as far as possible—we will argue on a psychodynamic basis—is a foundation of the intrapersonal and interpersonal balances of human organism, and thus, of psychological well-being and mental health.
>
> (Maraffa & Paternoster, 2016, p. 116)

The psychodynamic basis as observation point (Salas et al., 2018) is useful to better understand the therapist–patient interactions during the analytical session. That is, what is described as a narrative Self, even in the field of philosophy (Dennett, 1987; Goldie, 2012; Velleman, 2007), can be understood as a narrative thought that involves the narration (and signification) of past events through the current Self (as occurs in the psychoanalytic session). In this case, according to the last three authors cited, the narrative structure of the Self is not a list of events, but it gives coherence and meaning to the story through the emotional and affective involvement of the narrator. Quoting Maraffa and Paternoster (2016):

> Autobiographical reasoning is constitutive of narrative identity. It embeds personal memories in a culturally, temporally, causally, and thematically coherent life story; thus, in keeping with our argument in the third section, the life story format establishes and re-establishes the diachronic continuity of the Self.
>
> (Maraffa & Paternoster, 2016, p. 120)

The diachronic continuity of the Self is placed by these authors at the service of the autobiographic narrative, while no continuity is given to the Minimal Self.

As we will see later, the issue of Self-continuity will accompany the book and our reflection on psychopathology.

Considering the bonding between consciousness and the Self, Damasio (2018) introduces the ability to produce images (image-making) as the basis of subjectivity and consciousness, thus placing the importance of non-verbal narratives immediately next to the ability to translate the non-verbal into a linguistic code.

The characteristics of the Self such as non-verbal and pre-reflexive skills (memory, image creation, space–time categorization, gestural and mime affective exchange, emotional responses, etc.), and verbal skills (propositional and representational linguistic code) must therefore be understood not only in terms of evolution or development (transition from primitive forms to more evolved and competent forms of the Self) but as coexisting throughout human existence. As stated by De Bruins, Duing, and Gallagher:

> Any given self may consist of a variety of aspects, including (but not limited to) minimal experiential aspects and minimal embodied aspects, but also affective, intersubjective, cognitive, narrative, and extended/situated aspects (Gallagher, 2013). Importantly, this is not meant as an additive list of factors, but as components dynamically interrelated in a pattern or gestalt arrangement. Adjustments in one aspect will lead, via dynamical interactions, to modulations in others.
>
> (De Bruin et al., 2017, p. 112)

Facets of the Self: IV—Self-continuity and identity

Alongside the bodily, cognitive and affective characteristics of the Self introduced so far, we emphasize the central role of its continuity, Self-continuity (Northoff, 2017), as the core of identity development.

> Much attention has been given to the 'Synchronic Self', i.e. to the characteristics of the Self at a given moment, less to the 'Diachronic Self' or Self-continuity, i.e. to the time dimension of the Self ensured by the temporal features of spontaneous CMS (Cortical Midline Structures) neuronal activity. With their strong infra-slow power and long temporal durations, the CMS are ideally suited to encode and integrate information over long time scales. This process is supposed to mediate the encoding of external stimuli.
>
> (Northoff, 2017, p. 126)

Self-continuity is about memory. However, it is not the 'usual' kind of memory that is related to specific contents, e.g. cognitive memory in terms of information about these contents. Instead, contents seem to be encoded in terms of their underlying temporal features by seemingly corresponding temporal features in the CMS neural activity. The CMS neural activity thus seems to mediate a non-cognitive form of memory. As such, non-cognitive memory is apparently and predominantly based on temporal (and spatial) features of the CMS activity and its processes; we may speak of 'spatiotemporal memory'. In turn, this spatiotemporal memory may provide the basis for the more traditional notion of memory, that is, focused on specific contents or information—that is why it is referred to as 'cognitive memory' (Northoff, 2017).

Spatiotemporal memory connects both levels, the brain and psyche, by serving as their 'common currency' (Wolff et al., 2019). In turn, the spatio-temporal memory can be the very basis of Self-continuity and ultimately of identity, e.g. our personal identity throughout our whole lifetime.

Why single case reports—Introducing the clinical cases

Neuropsychodynamic psychiatry (Boeker et al., 2018), neuropsychoanalysis (Solms & Turnbull, 2011), and psychodynamic psychotherapy (Gabbard, 2005) currently attach great importance to the patients' internal world: fantasies, dreams, hopes, wishes, fears, impulses, self-images, perception of others, and psychological reactions to symptoms. Hence the crucial question: how can we exchange information about the different models of treatment?

The model of the three-dimensional neuropsychodynamic structure—defences, conflict, and structure—(Boeker et al., 2018) helps us to reflect on the psychopathologies presented through the psychoanalytic sessions. The clinical cases in the book show the influence of psychoanalysis through the authors who contributed most to its development (Wallerstein, 2002; Mills, 2005; Wachtel, 2008) and through the models related to the inclusion of affective neuroscience in psychoanalytic treatment (Spagnolo, 2018). The presentation of clinical cases is a practice widely used in psychoanalytic circles. However, it has never been well received in the field of research for many reasons, including: no possibility to generalize the individual clinical experience, small numbers, and subjectivity of the method (Flyvbjerg, 2006); all these context-dependent elements may not help to extrapolate context-independent elements and therefore generalize, as suggested by Salas et al. (2018):

> If we consider the dominant scientific paradigms, the reader may easily recognize the assumption that universal laws are true knowledge in science. Even though this logic may apply to fields such as physics or chemistry, it cannot be easily extrapolated to human behaviour. Human beings become experts on a task or activity, not by acquiring and manipulating context-independent knowledge or a set of abstract rules, but by progressively amassing a body of knowledge based on concrete interactions with the environment.
>
> (p. 65)

Perhaps, the issue is not the possibility to generalize the individual case, but rather it reflects the inherent difficulties in studying human behaviour. The studies of human beings (and therefore of psychopathology) sweep through their biography, behaviour, story, in other words, their subjectivity and the environment in which they live. From the point of view of individual development, this means integrating and representing aspects inherent to the Minimal Self, namely the basic form of the Self that is part of any experience, with increasingly complex forms of the Self, in which memory, cognitive skills and affects make it possible to link together different time points. In fact, the Self is not an isolated element of the individual mind, but it is always and continuously connected with the mind of others and with the environment in which it is rooted. Therefore, in the clinical presentations, we will also consider what brings together story, memory, and narration to make them more comprehensible.

After writing stories of other people for years, Inga Clendinnen (2000) writes her own story out of her fear of death, perhaps caught in the delirium of drugs. Her story is told through her memories, but these memories are romanticized (narrated) to hold together parts of the Self that otherwise would have appeared with their total existential discontinuity. The author outlines that the individual story, like the collective stories, narrated through the muddy reality of everyday life, makes the past familiar to us with its oddities and atrocities.

The existential discontinuity and continuity of the Self seems to rephrase the question of the Multiple Self–Unitary Self relation. This reflection may be reformulated to include the organization of defences, for example: what kind of emotional engagement (connection with the body) and affective engagement (connection with the object) is possible when the event (memory reconstruction) is inserted in a representative chain. Hence, what happens when this is not possible (representation/historicization of the event) due to traumas prior to the emergence of verbal experience (Mucci, 2018).

Does the narrative Self, through its contents, call for an iridescent Self that becomes assembled and disassembled to accommodate the variations of an event? Or, according to Bromberg (2011), is it a multiple Self that deals with the event in a different way without any reciprocal interaction? Perhaps this question should be raised not so much in relation to the structure of the Self, that we are investigating, but rather to a different context concerning the integration of the different information we receive, whether it is processed in a unitary form or not.

Conclusion

In reflecting on the environmental changes, we ask whether the ongoing transformations are to be included in the physiological and reassuring concept of slow and gradual biological evolution or in the more disturbing concept of evolutionary leaps, in line with Ramachandran (2011):

> It is a common fallacy to assume that gradual, small changes can only engender gradual, incremental results. But this is linear thinking, which seems to be our default mode for thinking about the world. This may be due to the simple fact that most of the phenomena that are perceptible to humans, at everyday human scales of time and magnitude and within the

limited scope of our naked senses, tend to follow linear trends. Two stones feel twice as heavy as one stone. It takes three times as much food to feed three times as many people. And so on. But outside of the sphere of practical human concerns, nature is full of nonlinear phenomena. Highly complex processes can emerge from deceptively simple rules or parts, and small changes in one underlying factor of a complex system can engender radical, qualitative shifts in other factors that depend on it.

(p. 22)

What then comes up of these individual and social transformations during the session? And how does the Self adapt to this? One of the characteristics of our consciousness (even the minimal one described by Metzinger (2005) as globality-constraint, presentationality-constraint, and transparency-constraint) is to be able to react to its own contents through a series of mental or bodily mechanisms that shape the whole experience we make/have of that event at that moment. Consciousness can direct the attention to select a detail and, if linked to a certain context, it becomes the fulcrum of a thought or memory that can be represented in an episode and be communicated. So, consciousness is an incredible machine capable of using completely unconscious and automatic (defensive) mechanisms to generate slices of consciousness (i.e. itself, or autopoiesis) that make us aware of the 'here and now' of a situation. Who is aware of what? Through these unconscious automatisms, the transparency of the Self (I don't have to think all the time, it's me who think, act, look, etc.) paves the way to consciousness; that is, it facilitates the selection of data to obtain information that feeds the awareness of the event/object at that moment. The Self acquires a temporal domain, more extensive than that used by consciousness, that is time travel through past, present and future:

> Such mental time travel with self-projection into past and future has been described as Episodic Simulation (ES) [...] ES can be characterized by mental time travel that makes it possible to project the own self and related events into time (i.e. past and future). The projection into time allows the self (and its related events) to detach or decouple itself from the specific point in time and the current environmental context.
>
> (Northoff, 2017, p. 126)

To conclude, the temporal dimension of the Self (from non-cognitive memories to the descriptive narrative dimension), the geometric dimension (I dwell in a geometric space, well defined by my own body and the external objects), the affective dimension (starting from infancy, I live experiencing the relationship with the others), the three axes that draw the 3D dimension of the Self, will be analyzed through the psychoanalytic treatment presented in the next chapters. Moreover, we will describe some aspects of the Self (Unity,

Continuity, Embodiment, Privacy, Social Embedding, Free Will, Self-Awareness) proposed by Ramachandran (2011):

> These seven aspects, like table legs, work together to hold up what we call the self. However, as you can already see, they are vulnerable to illusions, delusions, and disorders. The table of the self can continue to stand without one of these legs, but if too many are lost then its stability becomes severely compromised.
>
> (Ramachandran, 2011, p. 201)

At a closer look, these seven aspects still suggest something related to the ongoing changes in psychotherapy: if the number of possible forms, and hence transformations, of the Self increases through the continuous interaction with the analyst, the Self becomes more and more stable and increasingly predictable and foreseeable. This may allow the patient-therapist couple to better understand the symptoms and to better monitor the progress of the treatment.

References

Alcaro, A., Carta, S., & Panksepp, J. (2017). The affective core of the self: A neuro-archetypical perspective on the foundations of human (and animal) subjectivity. *Frontiers in Psychology*, 8 (1424):1–13.

Beebe, B., Lachmann, F., & Jaffe, J. (1997). Mother–infant interaction structures and presymbolic self- and object representations. *Psychoanalytic Dialogues, 7(2)*:133–182.

Beebe, B., & Lachmann, F. (1998). Co-constructing inner and relational processes: Self and mutual regulation in infant research and adult treatment. *Psychoanalytic Psychology, 15*:1–37.

Beebe, B., & Lachmann, F. (2003). The relational turn in psychoanalysis: A dyadic systems view from infant research. *Contemporary Psychoanalysis, 39*:379–409.

Boeker, H., Hartwich, P., & Northoff, G. (2018). *Neuropsychodynamic Psychiatry*. Switzerland: Springer Nature.

Bowlby, J. (1969). *Attachment and loss, Vol. I: Attachment*. New York: Basic Books.

Bromberg, M. P. (1994). 'Speak! that I may see you': Some reflections on dissociation, reality, and psychoanalytic listening. *Psychoanalytic Dialogues*, 4:517–547.

Bromberg, M. P. (2011). *The shadow of the tsunami and the growth of the relational mind*. London/New York: Routledge.

Clendinnen, I. (2000). *Tiger's Eye—A Memoir*. Melbourne: Text Publishing.

Cooper, A. M. (2006). *Contemporary psychoanalysis in America: Leading analysts present their work*. 1st Ed. New York: American Psychiatric Association Publishing.

Damasio, A. (1999). *The feeling of what happens*. New York: Harcourt Brace.

Damasio, A. (2010). *Self comes to mind. Constructing the conscious brain*. New York: Vintage.

Damasio, A. (2018). *The strange order of things*. New York: Pantheon Books.

De Bruin, L., Dings, R., & Gallagher S. (2017). The multidimensionality and context dependency of selves. *AJOB Neuroscience*, 8(2):112–114.

Dennett, D. C. (1987). *The intentional stance.* Cambridge, MA: MIT Press.

Dennett, D. C. (1991). *Consciousness explained.* Boston: Little, Brown and Co.

Dennett, D. (2005). *Sweet dreams.* Cambridge, MA: MIT Press.

Edelman, G. M. (1989). *The remembered present: A biological theory of consciousness.* New York: Basic Books.

Fairbairn, B. E., & Scharff, D. (1988/1994). *From instinct to self: Selected papers of W. R. D. Fairbairn.* Maryland: Aronson.

Flyvbjerg, B. (2006). Five misunderstandings about case study research. *Qualitative Inquiry,* 12(2):219–245.

Fonagy, P., Gergely, G., Jurist, E., & Target, M. (2004). *Affect regulation, mentalization, and the development of the self.* London: Karnac.

Freud, S. (1894a). *The neuro-psychoses of defence. S.E.,* 3:43–61. London: Hogarth.

Gabbard, G. O. (2005). *Psychodynamic psychiatry in clinical practice.* Washington, DC: American Psychiatric Publishing Inc.

Gallagher, S. (2000). Philosophical conceptions of the self: Implications for cognitive science. *Trends in Cognitive Sciences,* 4(1):14–21.

Gallagher, S. (2013). A pattern theory of self. *Frontiers in Human Neuroscience,* 7:443.

Goldie, P. (2012). *The mess inside: Narrative, emotion, and the mind.* New York: Oxford University Press.

Greenberg, J., & Mitchell, S. (1983). *Object relations in psychoanalytic theory.* Cambridge, MA: Harvard University Press.

Hohwy, J. (2007): The sense of self in the phenomenology of agency and perception. *Psyche,* 13(1): 1–20.

Huang, Z., Obara, N., Davis, H. H., Pokorny, J., & Northoff, G. (2016). The temporal structure of resting-state brain activity in the medial prefrontal cortex predicts self-consciousness. *Neuropsychologia,* 82:161–170.

Klein, M., Heimann, P., Isaacs, S., & Riviere, J. (1952). *Developments in psychoanalysis.* London: Hogarth Press.

Kohut, H. (1971). *The analysis of the self.* New York: International Universities Press.

Kohut, H. (1977). *The restoration of the self.* New York: International Universities Press.

Lester, D. (2012). A multiple self theory of the mind. *Comprehensive Psychology,* 1(5):1–11.

Lifton, R. J. (1993). *The Protean self.* New York: Basic Books.

Maraffa, M., & Paternoster, A. (2016). Disentangling the self. A naturalistic approach to narrative self-construction. *New Ideas in Psychology,* 40:115–122.

Metzinger, T. (2003). *Being No One. The Self-Model Theory of Subjectivity.* Cambridge, MA: MIT Press.

Metzinger, T. (2005). Precis being no one. *Psyche,* 11(5): 1–35.

Mills, J. (2005). A critique of relational psychoanalysis. *Psychoanalytic Psychology,* 228(2):155–188.

Mitchell, S. A. (1988). *Relational concepts in psychoanalysis: An integration.* Cambridge, MA: Harvard University Press.

Mitchell, S. A. (1992). True selves, false selves, and the ambiguity of authenticity. In N. J. Skolnick & S. C. Warshaw (Eds), *Relational perspectives in psychoanalysis* (pp. 1–20). Hillsdale: Analytic Press.

Mitchell, S. A. (1993). *Hope and dread in psychoanalysis.* New York: Basic Books.

Mitchell, S. A. (1995). Harry Stack Sullivan and interpersonal psychoanalysis. In: S. A.

Mitchell & M. Black (Eds), *Freud and beyond—a history of modern psychoanalytic thought* (pp. 60–84). New York: Basic Books.

Mitchell, S. A. (2000). *Relationality: From attachment to intersubjectivity.* Hillsdale, NJ: Analytic Press.

Modell, A.H. (1996). *The interface of psychoanalysis and neurobiology.* Boston Colloquium for Philosophy of Science—December 18, 1996, in Paper Presentation—The Poles of Health: Biological and Social approaches to Disordered Minds. Boston.

Mucci, C. (2018). *Borderline bodies.* London/New York: W W Norton& Company.

Neisser, U. (1967). *Cognitive psychology.* New York: Appleton-Century-Crofts.

Noë, A. (2004). *Action in perception.* Cambridge, MA: MIT Press.

Northoff, G. (2016). Is the self a higher-order or fundamental function of the brain? The 'basis model of self-specificity' and its encoding by the brain's spontaneous activity. *Cognitive Neuroscience,* 7(1–4):203–222.

Northoff, G. (2017). Personal identity and cortical midline structure (CMS): Do temporal features of CMS neural activity transform into 'self-continuity'? *Psychological Inquiry,* 28 (2–3):122–131.

Northoff, G. (2018). Self between brain and world: Neuropsychodynamic approach, social embedded brain and relational self. In H. Boeker, P. Hartwich, & G. Northoff (Eds), *Neuropsychodynamic Psychiatry.* Switzerland: Springer Nature.

Palombo, J. (2018). *The neuropsychodynamic treatment of self deficit.* London/New York: Routledge.

Panksepp, J. (1998b). *Affective Neuroscience: The Foundations of Human and Animal Emotions.* New York: Oxford University Press.

Panksepp, J., & Northoff, G. (2009). The trans-species core SELF: The emergence of active cultural and neuro-ecological agents through self-related processing within subcortical-cortical midline networks. *Consciousness and Cognition,* 18(1):193–215.

Panksepp, J., & Biven, L. (2012). *Archaeology of Mind: Neuroevolutionary origins of human emotions.* New York: Norton.

Panksepp, J., Asma, S., Curran, G., Gabriel R., & Greif, T. (2012). The philosophical implications of affective neuroscience. *Journal of Consciousness Studies,* 19 (3–4):6–48.

Ramachandran, V. (2011). *The tell-tale brain.* New York London: W. W. Norton & Company.

Salas, E., Casassus, M., & Turnbull, H. O. (2018). The Case study in neuropsychoanalysis: a bridge between the objective and the subjective. In R. Spagnolo (Ed), *Building bridges. The impact of neuropsychoanalysis on psychoanalytic clinical session* (pp. 55–87). London/New York: Routledge.

Schore, A. N. (2003a). *Affect regulation and the repair of the Self.* New York/London: W W Norton & Company.

Schore, A. N. (2003b). *Affect dysregulation and disorders of the Self.* New York/ London: W W Norton & Company.

Solms, M., & Turnbull, O. H. (2011). What Is Neuropsychoanalysis? *Neuro-Psychoanalysis,* 13(2): 133–145.

Spagnolo, R. (2018). *Building bridges. The impact of neuropsychoanalysis on psychoanalytic clinical session.* London/New York: Routledge.

Stern, D. N. (1985). *The interpersonal world of the infant.* New York: Basic Books.

Stolorow, R. D., & Atwood, G. (1992). *Contexts of being: The intersubjective foundations of psychological life.* Hillsdale: Analytic Press.

Strawson, G. (1997): The self. *Journal of Consciousness Studies,* 4:405–428.

Sullivan, H.S., & Kernberg, O. F. (1976). *Object relations theory and clinical psychoanalysis.* New York: Jason Aronson.

Tronick, E. (2007). *The neurobehavioral and social-emotional development of infants and children.* New York/London: W W Norton & Company.

Tsakiris, M. (2010). My body in the brain: a neurocognitive model of body ownership. *Neuropsychologia,* 48(3):703–712.

Velleman, J. D. (2007). *Self to self: Selected essays.* New York: Cambridge University Press.

Wachtel, P. (2008). *Relational theory and the practice of psychotherapy.* New York: The Guilford Press.

Wallerstein, R. (2002). The trajectory of psychoanalysis: a prognostication. *International Journal of Psychoanalysis,* 83:1247–1267.

Wilson, A. D., & Golonka, S. (2013). Embodied cognition is not what you think it is. *Frontiers in Psychology,* 4(58): 1–13.

Winnicott, D. W. (1965). *Maturational processes and the facilitating environment: Studies in the theory of emotional development.* London: Hogarth Press.

Wolff, A., Di Giovanni, D.A., Gómez-Pilar, J., Nakao, T., Huang, Z., Longtin, A., & Northoff, G. (2019). The temporal signature of self: Temporal measures of resting-state EEG predict self-consciousness. *Human Brain Mapping,* 40(3):789–803.

Zahavi, D. (2006). *Subjectivity and selfhood: Investigating the first-person perspective.* Cambridge, MA: MIT Press.

Chapter 1

Building up time and space

Self-embodiment

Our body is always with us. Even when we are not aware of its presence, it manifests itself through our gestures; it is noticeable when we speak, when our facial expressions follow the emotional dialogue, or when we are fulfilling a task and our postures change to find a new spatial arrangement, without discontinuing what we are doing. The body is present in the spatial concepts related to its displacement in space that express both the idea of movement and embodied metaphors (Lakoff & Johnson, 1980) such as, for example, up/down, in front of/behind, metaphors of goal achievement, and mood changes.

Each body has different cognitive/affective abilities according to its physical characteristics. The way in which eyes, hands, legs, and other body parts, are shaped determines the type of knowledge we acquire of the world, which is different in human beings with respect to non-human beings.

The body is 'situated' in the world (Varela et al., 1991) and actively tries out different spatial, and also temporal, configurations and navigations in the world (Noë, 2004; Gallagher, 2005a; Gallagher, 2017), through its shape (body features). The body's situatedness in the world is the basis of our experience of the world, including of our own body as part of that very same world:

> By the term embodied, we emphasize two points: first, cognition depends upon the kinds of experience that come from having a body with various sensorimotor capacities; second, these individual sensorimotor capacities are themselves embedded in a more encompassing biological, psychological and cultural context.
>
> (Varela et al., 1991, p. 172)

Our body supposedly accompanies us everywhere, it is always there where we are, and it is the origin of our being in the world. But in which way is the body linked to the Self thus creating knowledge?

DOI: 10.4324/9781003221876-2

The body knows, decides, chooses, and responds to internal and external stimuli; without taking all this into consideration, the mind is seen as 'disembodied', conjuring up the eternal dualism of Descartes' pilot (thought-generating representational/symbolic systems) who steers the body-container. Therefore, in order to speak of embodiment, 'mental representations need to be grounded in perception and action; they cannot be a free-floating system of symbols'.

(Dijkstra & Zwaan, 2014, p. 296)

Embodiment involves both the perceptual system, deemed as an integrated multisensory system, and, the Self, as a form of embodied memory, that goes beyond perceptions of peripheral events, and extensively maps them into the body inner states; we call this 'Self-embodiment'.

We need to distinguish different concepts related to the body. According to Assoun (1987/2015), *Körper* is the body structure or anatomy that can be wounded or injured; *Leib* is the root of the living body and *Leiche* is the dead body, the corpse. However, *Körper* means the body's physical, and biological attributes; it grounds us in the world through the lived body, namely the *Leib*.

These definitions can be traced to Husserl (1913/1989), who exhaustively discussed the phenomenology of *Körper* as the body-as-an-object and of *Leib* as the body-as-a-subject. *Leib* is the lived body that not only transcends the sense of our being in the world (Merleau-Ponty, 2012) but that goes beyond the boundaries of the body as *Körper*, thus opening up the biological dimension of the living to the dimension of existence of Self as distinct from others (Self–Other dimension, J. P. Sartre, 1956).

Thus, *Körper* and *Leib* are intertwined and they both own and share what is called the Self. In this connection, according to psychoanalysis, the Self is the unconscious link 'glueing' together these different concepts of the body, *Körper* and *Leib*.

It is extremely difficult to define the 'body' in psychoanalysis because there is always something which is neither limited to the body nor to the mind; in fact, in 1917, Freud wrote to Groddeck: 'Certainly, the unconscious is the proper mediator between the somatic and the mental, perhaps the long-sought "missing link". Yet, because we have seen this at last, should we no longer see anything else?' (Groddeck, 1977, p. 38).

Accepting the possibility of being able 'to see something else' or at least to find 'this missing link', we now consider the unconscious processes as the ongoing work of the living body to integrate perceptions (both internal and external) in a broader context of meaning, which yields memories and sub-jectivation of the Self beyond its objective basis in the body, i.e. *Körper*. Hence, in the unconscious dimension, both memories and Self are embodied. If the unconscious subjectivation of Self and body is blocked or dysfunctional, we will encounter abnormal manifestations of the Self and the body in both the unconscious and consciousness, i.e. symptoms.

Is the minimum unit (Minimal Self) of the individual an irreducible mind–body, *Körper–Leib*, lump? If we introduce the emergence of the Self as bodily Self, the body marks the construction of the individual bodily Self with its proprioceptive, sensory, affective, characteristics. According to Mucci (2018), the individual develops as a complex body–mind–brain system; it is important to add to this construction a further degree of complexity since the body keeps a double inscription into the brain (Solms & Panksepp, 2012): a cortical inscription of the body like an object (external body), an object among other objects with different motor and perceptive parts; a sub-cortical inscription of the subjective body (internal body). This has nothing to do with the perception of the body-as-an-object, but with the experience of the body as a subject, that is with affects, with 'being' and subjectivation.

Thanks to this subjective, affective body, we perceive that we are our body, that we have a body:

> Living my body means more than being aware of my body or having a body image […] This doesn't mean that I experience myself exclusively as a body […] The natural engineering of the human body […] allows us to generate narratives and metaphors that lead us beyond the simple Self-body equation. I am this body and I am more than this body.
>
> (Gallagher, 2005b, p. 8)

Self-continuity

Following Richardson and Chemero (2014), we are introducing a brain in a body, in an environment that can comprise a heterogeneous, complex dynamical system. This system exhibits emergent behaviour, which is Self-organized since it does not result from a controlling component agent. Further:

> Dynamical systems that exhibit this kind of emergent, context-dependent behaviour are often referred to as softly assembled systems in that the behavioural system reflects a temporary coalition of coordinated entities, components, or factors […] For softly assembled, interaction-dominant dynamical systems, system behaviour is the result of interactions between system components, agents, and situational factors, with these inter-components or inter-agent interactions altering the dynamics of the component elements, situational factors and agents themselves.
>
> (Richardson & Chemero, 2014, p. 40)

We know that in a non-linear complex dynamical system, the output is not the sum of its weighted inputs, i.e. it cannot be broken down by the predictable behaviour of its single components. Therefore, according to this analysis, it is impossible to separate and isolate the body (brain) from the Self; instead, their interaction suggests that: 'Non-linear time-series analysis is essential for understanding how the ordered regularity of human behaviour and cognition can emerge and be maintained' (Richardson & Chemero, 2014, p. 41).

The brain's spontaneous activity and its link to experience and the living body (Northoff & Stanghellini, 2016) suggests that this cerebral activity is independent of specific externally directed processes and stimuli. In a resting state, the brain consistently and hence dynamically constructs spatiotemporal features, with an ongoing process of change that integrates the internal and proprioceptive inputs from the body within a larger spatiotemporal framework. The subjectivation of Self and body may then be traced to the dynamics of this continuous spatiotemporal construction:

> This leads to postulate what can be described as the temporal hypothesis of the 'lived body'. We tentatively postulate that the difference between objective vs. lived body in experience is closely related to the resting state's spatiotemporal features during internally-directed processing: the better the body's intero-and proprioceptive input is integrated into the resting state's ongoing temporal structure during its internally-directed processing, the higher the degree of subjective experience of the body as 'lived body' as distinguished from the experience of a merely 'objective body'.
>
> (Northoff & Stanghellini, 2016, p. 9)

How can we support that idea on empirical grounds? We assume that one central feature of this spatiotemporal construction and embedding of the Self and the body is temporal continuity which results in Self-continuity. This is in line with recent empirical data. On the basis of a functional connectivity analysis of a large resting-state data set, Murray (Murray et al., 2012; Murray et al., 2015) showed that the anterior midline regions, as well as the anterior insula, form a 'Self-network' in the resting state. This neural overlap between the Self and the resting state implies that the spontaneous activity of the CMS (Cortical Midline Structures) plays a central role, thus making it well suitable for mediating the Self and its continuity. Self-continuity is central to human life and allows us to understand how the *ordered regularity of human behaviour and cognition can emerge and be maintained. Temporal* low-frequency fluctuations and *spatial* functional connectivity patterns characterize the resting-state activity of the brain. The temporal structure plays an important role in bridging the gaps between different discrete points in time. By linking together the neural activities at different discrete points in time, the brain's intrinsic activity acquires a certain degree of temporal continuity (Northoff, 2012).[1]

Moreover, a full neurobiological account of the body–Self dimension should include how the interoceptive and exteroceptive bodily information is combined to form the conscious experience of being a person (Aspell et al., 2013; Heydrich et al., 2018).

Due to the ongoing space–time construction of this spontaneous activity, it can continuously integrate interoceptive and exteroceptive bodily inputs, thus creating bodily continuity as one hallmark of the *Leib* as distinguished from the *Körper*.

Typical hallmarks of Self are Self-identification, Self-location, First-Person Perspective (Furlanetto et al., 2013).

We now add Self-continuity to that list.

Out-of-body experiences

To illustrate the relevance of Self-continuity, we introduce the clinical case of disembodied experience. Such disorder is defined as Autoscopic Phenomena (AP) or illusory own-body perceptions mainly in three forms: autoscopic hallucinations (AH), out-of-body experiences (OBE), and heautoscopy (HAS) (Blanke & Mohr, 2005).

These disorders share the experience of being/seeing the body in an extra personal space.

> During autoscopic hallucinations, a second own body is seen without any changes in bodily Self-consciousness. During out-of-body experiences, the second own body is seen from an elevated perspective and location associated with disembodiment. During heautoscopy, subjects report strong Self-identification with the second own body, often associated with the experience of existing at and perceiving the world from two places at the same time.
>
> (Heydrich & Blanke, 2013, p. 790)

We are interested in the third form of autoscopic phenomenon, namely heautoscopy, in which the patient cannot decide the location of the body (bi-location) as if he is experiencing to exist in two places at the same time (Heydrich & Blanke, 2013).[2]

In heautoscopy, the body duplication is not only an image or a visual hallucination (as in autoscopic hallucinations) because the Self can be experienced in the position of the physical body or in the duplicate body (simultaneously or in alternation) and the subject is not able to report where the Self is localized (Ionta et al., 2011).

To sum up:

> The three forms of AP differ with respect to the three phenomenological characteristics of disembodiment, perspective and autoscopy. Whereas there is no disembodiment in AH and always disembodiment in OBEs, subjects with HAS generally do not report clear disembodiment, but are often unable to localize their Self. Thus, in some patients with HAS, the Self is localized either in the physical body or in the autoscopic body, and

sometimes even at multiple positions. Accordingly, the visual-spatial perspective is body-centered in AH, extracorporeal in OBE, and at an extracorporeal and body-centered position in HAS.

(Blanke & Mohr, 2005, p. 187)

From the neurological point of view, these cases differ in terms of occipital or temporal brain lesions and in right or left-brain lesions (Blanke & Mohr, 2005; Ionta et al., 2011; Anzellotti et al., 2011). The temporal parietal junction (TPJ) and the posterior insula seem to be differently involved with the OBE and HAS disorders, respectively right/left involvement (Blanke & Mohr, 2005; Ionta et al., 2011). In these disorders, the Self is not tied to the constraints imposed by the body.

Where is the Self located during such experiences? Outside the bodily boundaries? Where is the physical body located? Does the human mind allow for localization in more than one places at the same time?

(Furlanetto et al., 2013, p. 1)

In *The Unconscious* Freud (1915a) reminds us that the unconscious exerts an intense plastic influence on somatic processes, which is never reached through a conscious act. Most mental processes that see the body as a protagonist (like procedural memories) are unconscious. Thus, the body is continuously on stage, a visible object that defines a presence. If the body and the mind do not proceed together, what happens to the structure of the Self? Typically, the body marks the time of the human existence through ageing; the body carries the signs of the past on the surface that is exposed to the other, but only the Self can keep together past, present and future. We can use another lexicon and say that the body is immanent to the mind and goes beyond the knowledge available to the mind, but the mind too continuously transcends the body by creating itself (the concept of autopoiesis). Sometimes, these references are not necessarily connected to the body, even though the body shapes and informs the mind. Here we are in the field of 'disembodiment'. At this point, we want to introduce AX in psychoanalytic treatment twice a week.

AX clinical case: Space and time dislocation

AX is a 35-year-old patient with the unpleasant sensation of being here and there at the same time or of not fully recognizing himself in the present moment (here and now). During the consultation, he says:

I feel out of space and time. If you ask me what time it is, what day or month it is, and where I am now, I perfectly know the answer. But it is as if I'm elsewhere, as if there's another me somewhere else, but I know that it's always me. And while I'm doing something, I know that I'm the one who is doing it, but at the same time I perceive myself elsewhere as if I wasn't acting at that moment. So, I say to myself: come back here, this is who you are and you are doing this thing; but for a few minutes I'm elsewhere and I have no contents. I only know that I'm elsewhere and not here.

Sometimes, he has sudden flashes of himself in the past; other times he is totally lost in the new space. He checks his health (by MNR, EEG, ECG, and so on) but everything is fine. He goes on and on describing what has been happening to him in the last two months: he no longer feels his body. He has no words to describe this feeling, but he tentatively says: '*My body is not here with me where I am, it is somewhere else*', and turns to look back to a distant place.

In order to deal with this situation, he pinches his skin, feels his pulse, counts his heartbeats, performs different workouts so as to momentarily perceive his body, even though he still experiences the strange feeling that his body is not with him, but elsewhere.

He talks about his longstanding concern for his health and about his pervasive and sometimes uncontrollable anxiety. When he feels that his body is not with him, he does not manage to perceive the essential sensations we take for granted.

Am I cold, hungry, full? I don't know. It's terrible, not only is my body elsewhere and not with me, but even when it is here with me (he is scratching and pinching his skin), I don't understand it.

We decide to meet regularly twice a week since the subject does not have any obvious organic issues.

Spatiotemporal view: Brief consideration on psychopathology

His symptoms have been interpreted in different ways: generalized anxiety disorder, panic disorder, dissociative disorder, out-of-body experience or, more in general, autoscopic experience.

What is going on in this case? We recall that the body and the Self are subjectivized by being integrated and embedded within the brain's spontaneous activity and its continuous construction of a spatiotemporal matrix. Time and space are here constructed in a dynamic way; that is, they provide a connection between different points in past, present, future time and space, and space points. This dynamic time-space construction makes it possible to continuously integrate the different inputs from the body and the Self, thus linking, connecting, and glueing them up. The dynamics of the brain's spontaneous activity is thus transferred to the Self and the body, so they become 'spatiotemporalized' and thereby 'dynamicised' if we wish to say so. In our experience, such dynamization and spatiotemporalization accounts for the presence of the Self and the *Leib* (as distinguished from the *Körper*).

Our patient suffers from the absence of these experiences. His Self is no longer experienced as continuously present and his body experience is no longer anchored in specific time-space coordinates; it remains out of time and space, as he says. We assume that the integration of the various interoceptive and exteroceptive inputs from his body, i.e. the *Körper*, are no longer integrated within the ongoing construction of time and space by his brain's spontaneous activity. Consequently, the *Körper* can no longer be transformed into a *Leib*, which triggers his anxiety as his *Körper* is not integrated and linked to his Self. And he can shift the *Körper* around, like any objective object, across different points in time and space. He clearly refers to that and reports this experience as being 'out of time and space'.

However, we assume that his disorder goes deeper beyond his impaired spatiotemporal integration and embedding of his body's inputs. We suppose that the construction of his time and space is altered by his consistent experience of possible discontinuation in the presence of his Self, namely, he lapses when his Self, the experience of his Self, remains absent. This means that his spatiotemporal construction too must be somehow discontinued and thus become fragmented. That is revealed in his experience or consciousness of a temporally discontinuity of his Self with lapses of absence between moments of presence. Hence, the temporal discontinuity of his spontaneous activity's space–time construction may be transformed into the experience of the temporal discontinuity of his Self on the mental level, showing up as lapses of absence of his Self.

From the treatment diary

Disembodiment

The sessions reveal that AX consistently wakes up at night out of his fear of having to go through his day, knowing he will never be totally present. He is afraid of these sudden interruptions of his presence. He has a strong desire to be alone, as already happened many years ago (when he was about 16 years old), when he failed an exam. When he is talking about the details of this failure, he gets disoriented. He feels that time collapses around this narrative, as if it is happening right now, like a *déjà vu* or a dream. I ask him some questions about being 'here and now' with me in this room and he responds promptly and vigilantly.

My first work proposal was to analyze this double time frame (or double reality, as he calls it) in which things happen in parallel. The analysis of this double time frame immediately reveals his experience of displacement in space.

When he moves from one place to another, from home to work, from one room to another room, he gets lost because he feels he does not know where his body is, whether it is in the old space or in the new space. At that moment, he does not know in which space he should live. When he is rapidly moving around, he is overwhelmed by this feeling of emptiness and does not know where his body is. Immediately afterwards, being out of this state, he feels anguished because he has not been able to master space or time. He associates this anguish with the panic attack he had when he was 13 years old. This panic attack led him to flee from where he was and run towards home.

AX has not lost his ability to identify himself with his physical body. Sometimes he loses the First-Person Perspective (i.e. *'I have nothing in my mind; I don't know what I feel and what I experience'*). He manages to control his anxiety and to calm down by updating the state of his Self whatever he does, namely his daily activities; instead, disperceptive states (i.e. time–space disorientation, strange sensations, bi-location) appear less controllable. Probably these disperceptive states are not linked to specific conflictual contents of the mind, but apparently represent discontinuity states of the Self, experienced as splits and lacks.

Indeed, when he feels disembodied, he does not feel fear or anguish and his mind is not inhabited by images. Usually he says:

> *These are strange, distorted perceptions, but, when someone calls me from the outside, I wake up (I come back). I pull myself up and then I realize even more that I was not in that body here, I was somewhere else, I don't know where. I have no thoughts or images or memories, while I am there …*

Instead, when we talk about the contents of his anxieties and phobias, it is possible to work on his defences, through dreams for example.

Anchoring points

His dreams are flashes with well-defined images, often, anchored to a specific affect, in which we can recognize the Self (location, agency, ownership, and so on). Going 'in and out of his body', without knowing is whereabouts, wears him down, and the day seems very long to him. He thinks he will leave his job and remain locked up in his familiar room.

By working on getting 'in and out of his body', he learns to recognize a sort of 'depersonalization aura' and finds out some fixed points to anchor himself in space and time. We call these points *'my anchoring points'*. If he has safe and recognizable *anchoring points*, he can reset the incoming sensations and reconfigure himself through these landmarks. For example, he tells about one day at work when the situation got totally out of hand:

> *It's like having a different vision of yourself in which you don't recognize yourself. It's a physical sensation, I'm not myself physically and I don't know where I am. The situation got out of hand; I couldn't control it. A*

colleague yelled at me and I promptly and perfectly came back to myself.
He gave me the coordinates to get me back into the environment.

Through his colleague, he updates the system: he turns it off and on again
(that he calls '*my reset*'). But this 'reset' does not always work and often he
has to walk for miles and miles chasing himself. This means he does not have
any space–time landmarks. So, we introduce this intricate idea: the space
inhabited by him is always the same, managed with different time frames.

In fact, space is time as he used to repeat to himself: now I do this then I do
that, then something else and so on. His mental time frame comes through his
schedules. The space (the places inhabited by him) is always physically the same,
but the time (spent inside these places) gives to them a different configuration
according to different commitments. He says:

> *It's terrible because I change together with space and time, and I'm a different*
> *person, I'm another person, I perceive myself differently and I don't recognize*
> *myself. It's like being continuously changeable, or it is as if there was an*
> *objective time marked by things to do and a subjective time of my own in*
> *which I'm not in this objective space and time.*

This quote clearly illustrates he is lacking the subjectivation of *Körper* and
Self given by the ongoing space–time construction of his brain's spontaneous
activity. Brain, *Körper*, and Self are no longer integrated and embedded. They
are like three distinct entities, side-by-side with no interconnection and
exchangeable locations in time and space.

The different space–time points where the Self and the body are located are
no longer connected by some kind of underlying spatial and temporal continuity; therefore, they remain purely objective without becoming subjective.
Consequently, the patient experiences his Self and his body as mere objects
(rather than in a subjective way), as they are detached from the subjective
time-space construction of his brain's spontaneous activity.

All of this is not unconscious, but it seems to be a clash between two states of
consciousness. Our work on space–time–continuity allows us to shift the attention from the body (*Körper*) to consciousness, since he puts himself up saying:

> *Come on, pull yourself up, now this is going away, and you'll find yourself,*
> *just wait. I'm fighting against a terrible reality that makes me perceive*
> *that: I'm not here; my body is somewhere else and not here with me.*

At the same time, we analyze two types of anxiety: the anticipatory anxiety
and the anxiety linked to the disembodiment. When the content of the session brings out his anxieties, we can further elaborate on these features of
his inner life. I work to allow him to recognize these two types of anxiety
pervading him: the anticipatory anxiety he feels when he has to start

working or take on a responsibility role, due to which he anticipates time; and the anxiety that comes when he realizes to be elsewhere, that his body is not there with him and that he has to return to a reality dimension (objective space–time).

He experiences the discontinuity of his Self through this second form of anxiety. How can consciousness fix this discontinuity? He says:

> The straight line is the simplest way to join two dots. Moving a lot triggers the muscles and the breath can follow their rhythm and be tuned to the pace … I go slow, I slow everything down and in about fifteen minutes I'm present to myself and I can start the day. It is a geometric pattern that I have lost and I no longer find the coordinates of the body and mind together. If I let myself go and move away from this pattern, I feel dizzy and absent-minded and I'm no longer there.

He is not afraid of the contents or of the objects that belong to his internal world; he is afraid of losing this pattern. Once, he gave himself another pattern (a memo with what he had planned in the morning with maps of well-defined schedules and spaces in which he wrote his actions).

He lost this pattern after another failure of the stationery shop he was running. And he ended locked up in his room.

The thoughtless body

Through the rhythm and continuity of the setting (his new anchoring points), he can figure new scenarios where to act without getting scared. *What am I thinking about while I'm elsewhere?* This insight brings out a lot of old memories and images:

> Everything is mine. I'm not split, but I feel it doesn't belong to me. It's as if someone else had lived it, it's not me and this then scares me and I say to myself: come back here, it's you. But I don't understand: is it my body that is somewhere else, so I can't attribute my thoughts to it? Or is it the mind that is elsewhere?

The frustration generated by being rejected by a young woman and his tendency to withdraw, locking himself up in his room, makes it easy for him to talk about his social inadequacy and his relational isolation. It is like living in a small comfort zone (his room, his workplace, his therapy room) without ever integrating them into a continuous emotional experience.

I suggest a new working-through oriented hypothesis: since he goes on without integrating anything and erasing, what happens if 'the erased part' of himself returns as a 'thoughtless body located somewhere else' because his thoughts have been cancelled?

The re-appropriation of a 'thoughtless body' brings his attention back to his unpleasant interoceptive aspects such as shaking, nausea, a disgusting feeling of being dirty, as he describes:

> *For example, the other day while I was going from one assignment to another, I chatted with a young woman and then I felt shaking, I was no longer in me, I couldn't work. I felt so twice in the past when I suffered two great frustrations (related to education and work). At that time, I couldn't look at myself in the face. I couldn't close my eyes because I didn't see myself there, with me. It was as if my body wasn't there with me and I couldn't see it anymore.*

I think to myself about his difficulty of getting in touch with desire and of managing frustrations and failures. Furthermore, I know he works by cutting (discontinuity) and by failing to integrate (First-Person Perspective). The restriction of space and time, i.e. living in the comfort zone, means restriction (coarctation and shrinking) of the structure of the Self. The square metre of 'comfort zone', built on avoidance, works by constraining all the functions of his Self.

In the meantime, he keeps talking of this young woman who suddenly disappeared:

> *On my way home I felt the strong desire to turn myself off. But this time, after all the work done, I didn't know how to turn the system off. I was sad and I felt sad much longer. The day after, I was absent all day long. I was 'in and out' of myself the whole day. I was agitated and I touched my body many times to feel it, in order to make sure it was there with me. After she disappeared, I wish to abandon every relationship.*

This case also shows that spatiotemporal integration and embedding go beyond the body. By integrating interoceptive stimuli from the body, with exteroceptive stimuli from the world, the former become virtually extended beyond themselves, reaching out to the world. This integration relates and situates our Self and body within the world. Our patient no longer exhibits this virtual expansion of his Self and body beyond his own physical body, the *Körper*, which leads him to withdraw from social relationships. He consequently feels better when he withdraws to his own room.

Embodiment

His disembodiment is still there even though his body acts differently: before he felt he was elsewhere and saw his body somewhere else; now he feels his body there with him; even when he sees it elsewhere, he feels that it is there with him and he touches it just to be sure.

It's as if my mind is telling me, you're feeling this way, but then it (the mind) goes away. It's as if I turn off on one side and turn on to the other side. The dirt I was talking about is an alteration of reality. As if reality contaminates me and forces me to inhabit it. I feel that altered reality is not my reality. It is like being altered because even reality is altered. The difference with the past (disembodiment phase) *is that now I feel everything as less harmful and these moments are not so frequent.*

I do not say anything about Self bi-location, partial disembodiment, changing in his First-Person Perspective, and so on. I point out some features of the Self through a metaphor. So, I introduce the glass transparency metaphor to what has been said so far in a year of therapy.

Usually we do not do any extra work to keep the Self separated from reality. Its transparency facilitates our thought about reality. In this case, the Self is like a transparent and invisible glass. If it stained, I say, we immediately become aware of its presence: we see the glass between us and the external world; it marks a boundary. That stain on the glass/Self is what he calls:

The dirt I perceive, and I have to deal with, because I no longer know if it is internal or external. I thought, what about if I lose my consciousness and never come back to be me? Now I live with these two realities, I'm simultaneously in two places. I wait for it to go away and I come back to be me.

The dirt he feels is his deformed reality but also his deformed Self that misperceives reality. If the glass is transparent, he does not perceive any boundaries with the external world; he looks out from the inside and vice versa without barriers. If it is dirty, he perceives the presence of the glass (barrier) and the differences between the internal and external world. We elaborate this metaphor over several sessions and, at last, we penetrate into his concerns as well as in the structure of his Self. This entails keeping his Self tuned with the internal/external world and, in the meantime, we restore its spatiotemporal frame. One of my comments on this aspect:

Dirt is also the worries that come and distort the perception of reality. You see yourself and reality as two separate and different things. You see yourself outside and not inside and you no longer know if you are looking from the inside or from the outside.

This new sensitivity to the value of the boundaries makes the absence (a week) of the therapist very difficult to bear. '*I lost the metaphor, I lost my anchoring points and above all, he says, I felt sick*'. During this week, he explains to me, all his internal organs hurt, his body was sick, he was in great pain. He worked trying to pretend he had nothing, but he felt disoriented. He was totally alienated; his thought was always elsewhere, without a way out.

I was clear-headed, but at the same time I answered automatically. This time my mind was somewhere else, with my body somewhere else, and I was like in a dream, the part that was there was not me. Then I came back to be me. It was a very strong feeling of alienation. When I was alienated, the pain disappeared. I did some more work, dragging myself because I no longer knew if I was the one working on that assignment or not. I walked for an hour in the rain. The rain on my body helped me reconnect with myself.

The therapist was absent for a while and every day something happened to him. He lost the landmarks created by the rhythm of the sessions and by this physical space. Since he was able to recognize the boundaries of the Self, he got afraid of his internal and external world because he could not blend them anymore. He had this dream:

I was dreaming of a young woman I was dating, who made me feel good. And then I have a dream where I climb up using my hands. I did not feel tired; it's a physical sensation. It's real. Before I dreamed of falling planes, now I constantly dream of climbing stairs, mountains, roller coasters, etc., but always using my hands. Feeling my hands climbing. I feel my fingers … grasping.

I connect our separation with the relapse of his symptoms. I put forward the assumption that his (perceived and real) body belongs to him even in the dream dimension and generates fatigue and discomfort since he has to deal with it. He adds, about our separation:

It was like receiving a punch in the head that makes you understand you're not adequate, and you'll always be disabled, and you need the support of the other. You try to detach yourself from this, to say it's not mine, but you cannot, and you become anxious.

My suggestion:

We can call this alienation, detachment, avoidance, anxiety; it does not matter for our working through. I would like just to remind you that you had an imaginary friend for decades. Do you remember that? He has been supportive. As soon as he disappeared, your disembodiment appeared.

And for the first time, he conjures up the onset of his out-of-body experience:

When I first had this feeling, I reacted wishing to lock myself up in the room, in the dark, and to never leave from there again. I was scared to see myself somewhere else. It's as if I entered a time and space that has been created together with detachment and I live two parallel realities. Now I'm confused because sometimes I have my point of view and my time, sometimes I have the other. And this week, in which you were absent, has brought back all the sensations of that time, all the bad feelings; very strong feelings, as if I refused the reality in which I must live. So, I stayed at home in bed. I just wanted to be shut off in the dark. Then once everything is over and I return into my body, the body feels tired as if it has received a major blow. It's like a wound that never heals. You feel so much energy that it makes you explode, and you go somewhere else. And then I realize it, I clench my teeth, my hands sweat, and I say to myself 'I can do it, I won't go crazy'. This was a dream of a long time ago: I was in front of the mirror and clenched my teeth not to get out of myself, not to go crazy; I made strange moves, strange faces, struggle to avoid splitting.

I notice the structure of the verbs between past and present, his effort to describe the body that escapes the grip of his mind going elsewhere and the attractive duplication (depersonalization and derealization) that brings peace by releasing all anguish. The analytical work, focused on re-inhabiting his body, leads him to deal with all his anxieties. Thanks to his experiential and narrative continuity, we can share my thoughts about the meaning of living in his own body and dealing with all his anxieties. At last he remarks:

Sometimes I perceive that it is this second part (the one elsewhere) that is acting and I feel out of the world; the part of me that is here is muffled, it perceives almost nothing, it's dazed. It seems as if you almost lose your senses; you're stunned; the outside world is muffled because it is the other that acts, not you. You don't know what to do and you don't know where you are, and you can't act.

I suggest that he should see places as spaces/places/situations differently from the geometric space that he maps. These spaces/places/situations also have a timestamp that characterizes and enlivens them when they are inhabited by living bodies (*Leib*). Dreams mix up places and spaces, deform, widen, compress. I propose this point of view to him:

Figuratively, this may also be the representation of your Self-structure as it faces reality. In fact, in the dream you say to yourself you have to clench your teeth not to go crazy even if that is all deformed.

He repeats:

I appreciated it and I try to protect myself from this, but integrating all this into one person, clenching my teeth ... it's not easy to be so vigilant about oneself.

Avoidance is not whatever is not chosen; I clarify to him that sometimes we call this adaptation; the following night he had a recurring dream but with a different outcome:

> *I used to close all the doors of my car to bar a young woman/thief from getting in (repetitive dream), but in this dream I don't close the one next to me, so the young woman gets in (new outcome). I'm not scared. We start chatting. She was a beautiful person. I gave her a date and I went out with her; she was dressed as a bride, she was beautiful.*

When he woke up, he was happy, and he felt happy all day long. He explains to me the transformation taking place in the dream: he has always been afraid of everything and again, in the dream, he was about to shut himself off and about to succeed; but time fooled him, so he did not manage to close the car door. So, fear kicks in and he suddenly realizes that it is a beautiful thing/girl and that dealing with it/her would enrich his life.

Considerations about the treatment

In their paper on autoscopy, Anzellotti et al. (2011) introduce this topic by analyzing mythology. They elaborate on the myth of Narcissus by Ovid and Plautus; they go through the double, the Sosia, in Dostoevsky and Otto Rank, the '*doppelgänger*' in Richter, bringing out some considerations on the six types of autoscopic phenomena, based on phenomenological criteria.

The psychoanalytic literature is full of papers on mirroring, the double, depersonalization and derealization, splitting personality, and so on. We would like to go further and delve into the psychotherapy of 'out-of-body experience', considering the failure to integrate multisensory/temporospatial signals resulting in a breakdown of the spatial unity between the Self and the body (Anzellotti et al., 2011, p. 3).

We have included the last dream to show the intensity of transference (the object–relationship with the analyst), the dream-related transformations (different outcome, emotional transformation), the recognition of affects and concerns. We would elaborate more on that in the chapter on the Self and dreams.

However, without our work on the space–time structure of the patient's Self, namely the reconstruction of its continuity and its embodiment, we would have never had the opportunity to reach the contents of his mind generating the conflict, his defences and the meaning ascribed to them. The neuropsychodynamic perspective (Boeker et al., 2018), including the three-dimensional model, allows us to follow the variations involved in any psychotherapy.

> The three-dimensional neuropsychodynamic model of psychic disorders enables a better understanding of the link between emotional experience and neuronal mechanisms concerning the essential dimensions of the

human development, the mode of defence and compensation, the mode of conflict, and the mode of structure.

(Boeker et al., 2018, p. 89)

The course of AX's psychotherapy illustrates how the analytic work had an impact on the structure of his Self: from its minimal embodiment form (relocation to the body) to its space–time structure (continuity). Once its continuity was restored, we could work on anxiety (various types of anxiety) and its control/containment. Finally, having re-established the boundaries of his Self (Self agency, Self ownership, Self collocation), we started work on the recognition and re-signification of traumatic nuclei. Psychoanalytic tools (settings, free associations, listening, transference and countertransference, dream work) have been widely used in psychotherapy and can be found in the clinical description. We would like to outline some more theoretical elements.

What is the lesson we can derive from this case? *Körper* needs to be integrated and embedded within the subject's time-space constructions, i.e. in his brain's spontaneous activity. This makes it possible to subjectivize *Körper*, which then can be experienced as *Leib*. The same kind of subjectivation applies to our Self, not only to out-of-body experiences. If the Self is not integrated and embedded within the space–time construction, including its temporal continuity, we will experience our Self in a discontinuous timeframe, with lapses of presence and absence. Hence, both the subjective Self and body/*Leib* are strongly based on spatiotemporalization; otherwise, we will have no access to their experience as such. Moreover, such spatiotemporalization extends beyond the physical body boundaries as it involves time and space around us, namely the social space and time. This is reflected in our patient's social withdrawal as well as in the importance of the therapeutic relation. Hence, subjectivation is not only spatiotemporal but, at the same time, also social and relational. We will analyze all this in greater depth in the third chapter.

Notes

1 Spatially, the brain's intrinsic activity can be characterized by different neural networks like the default-mode network (DMN), the cognitive-executive network (CEN), and the salience network (SN) (see Raichle et al., 2001; Menon, 2011; Raichle, 2009). The DMN concerns mainly cortical midline regions and the bilateral posterior parietal cortex (Buckner et al., 2008; Raichle et al., 2001). These regions seem to show high resting state activity, dense functional connectivity, and strong low frequency fluctuations (0.001–0.1 Hz) in the resting state, while the executive network comprises the lateral prefrontal cortex, the supragenual anterior cingulate, and posterior lateral cortical regions as core regions as they are involved in higher-order cognitive and executive functions. Finally, the salience network includes regions like the insula, the ventral striatum, and the dorsal anterior cingulate cortex that are associated with reward, empathy, intero/exteroception and other processes involving salience (see Menon, 2011; Wiebking et al., 2011; Yan et al., 2009). All three neural networks, DMN, CEN, and SN, show strong intrinsic

functional connectivity among their respective regions, while the functional connectivity to regions extrinsic to the respective network are usually much weaker in the resting state. That though can change during stimulus-induced activity when the relationship and thus the functional connectivity between the three networks are rebalanced (see Menon, 2011). (Northoff, 2012, p. 730)

2 Heautoscopy has also been linked to various neurological (Lippman, 1953; Blanke et al., 2004) and psychiatric conditions (Lukianowicz, 1958, 1963). These include temporal lobe epilepsy (Devinsky et al., 1989; Brugger et al., 1994; Tadokoro et al., 2006), neoplasia originating in the insular cortex (Brugger et al., 2006), typhoid fever (Fe´ re´, 1891; Menninger-Lerchenthal, 1946), migraine (Lippman, 1953), schizophrenia (Lukianowicz, 1963) and depression (Lukianowicz, 1958; Arenz, 2001). (Heydrich & Blanke, 2013, p. 792)

References

Anzellotti, F., Onofri, V., Maruotti, V., Ricciardi, L., Franciotti, R., Bonanni, L., Thomas, A., & Onofri, M. (2011). Autoscopic phenomena: Case report and review of literature. *Behavioral and Brain Functions*, 7(2):1–11.

Assoun, P.L. (1987/2015). *Corps et Symptôme. Leçons de psychanalyse*. Paris: Economica (first Ed. 1987).

Aspell, J.E., Heydrich, L., Marillier, G., Lavanchy, T., Herbelin., B., & Blanke, O. (2013). Turning body and self inside out: Visualized heartbeats alter bodily self-consciousness and tactile perception. *Psychological Science*, 24(12): 2445–2453.

Blanke, O., & Mohr, C. (2005). Out-of-body experience, heautoscopy, and autoscopic hallucination of neurological origin: Implications for neurocognitive mechanisms of corporeal awareness and self-consciousness. *Brain Research Reviews*, 50:184–199.

Boeker, H., Hartwich, P., Northoff, G. (2018). *Neuropsychodynamic psychiatry*. Switzerland: Springer Nature.

Dijkstra, K., & Zwaan, R., A. (2014). Memory and action. In L. Shapiro (Ed), *The Routledge Handbook of Embodied Cognition* (pp. 296–305). New York: Routledge.

Freud, S. (1915a). *The Unconscious*. S. E., 14:159–204. London: Hogarth.

Furlanetto, T., Bertone, C., & Becchio, C. (2013). The bilocated mind: new perspectives on Self-localization and Self-identification. *Frontiers in Human Neuroscience*, 7(71):1–6.

Gallagher, S. (2005a). *How the Body Shapes the Mind*. Oxford: Oxford University Press.

Gallagher, S. (2005b). Metzinger's matrix: Living the virtual life with a real body. *Psyche* 11(5): 1–8.

Gallagher, S. (2017). *Enactivist interventions: Rethinking the mind*. Oxford: Oxford University Press.

Groddeck, G. (1977). *The meaning of illness: Selected psychoanalytic writings including his correspondence with Sigmund Freud*. New York: International Universities Press Inc.

Heydrich, L., & Blanke, O. (2013). Distinct illusory own-body perceptions caused by damage to posterior insula and extrastriate cortex. *Brain, 136*:790–803.

Heydrich, L., Aspell, J.E., Marillier, G., Lavanchy, T., Herbelin., B., & Blanke, O. (2018). Cardio-visual full body illusion alters bodily Self-consciousness and tactile processing in somatosensory cortex. *Scientific Reports*, 8(9230):1–8.

Husserl, E. (1913/1989). *Ideas pertaining to a pure phenomenology and to a phenomenological philosophy, second book: Studies in the phenomenology of constitution* (R. Rojcewicz and A. Schuwer, Trans.). Dordrecht: Kluwer Academic Publishers, 1989.

Ionta, S., Heydrich, L., Lenggenhager, B., Mouthon, M., Fornari, E., Chapuis, D., Gassert, R., & Blanke, O. (2011). Multisensory mechanisms in temporo-parietal cortex support self-location and First-Person Perspective. *Neuron*, 70: 363–374.

Lakoff, G., & Johnson, M. (1980). *Metaphors we live by*. Chicago: University of Chicago Press.

Merleau-Ponty, M. (2012). *Phenomenology of perception* (D. A. Landes, Trans.). New York: Routledge.

Mucci, C. (2018). *Borderline bodies*. New York/London: W.W. Norton & Company.

Murray, R. J., Schaer, M., & Debban, M. (2012). Degrees of separation: a quantitative neuroimaging meta-analysis investigating Self-specificity and shared neural activation between Self- and other-reflection. *Neuroscience & Biobehavioral Reviews*, 36(3): 1043–1059.

Murray, R. J., Debban, M., Fox, P. T., Bzdok, D., & Eickhoff, S. B. (2015). Functional connectivity mapping of regions associated with Self- and other-processing. *Human Brain Mapping*, 36(4): 1304–1324.

Noë, A. (2004). *Action in perception*. Cambridge, MA: MIT Press.

Northoff, G. (2012). What the brain's intrinsic activity can tell us about consciousness? A tri-dimensional view. *Neuroscience and Biobehavioral Reviews*, 37:726–738.

Northoff, G., & Stanghellini, G. (2016). How to Link Brain and Experience? Spatiotemporal Psychopathology of the Lived Body. *Frontiers Human Neuroscience*, 10(172):1–15.

Richardson, M., J., & Chemero, A. (2014). Complex dynamical systems and embodiment. In L. Shapiro (Ed), *The Routledge handbook of embodied cognition* (pp. 38–50). New York: Routledge.

Sartre, J.P. (1956). *Being and nothingness: An essay on phenomenological ontology* (H. E. Barnes, Trans.). New York: Philosophical Library.

Solms, M., & Panksepp, J. (2012). The 'id' knows more than the 'ego' admits. *Brain Science*, 2: 147–175.

Varela, F.J., Thompson, E., & Rosch, E. (1991). *The embodied mind: Cognitive science and human experience*. Cambridge MA: MIT Press.

Chapter 2

The Self and the Other

One body two minds: The inclusion of the 'Other'

What happens to the construction of the Self when two subjects share the same body as in the case of conjoined twins, or in an extreme mother–father–child psychic symbiotic relationship?

We introduce some reflections on the construction of the Self related to the body–mind development in the case of dicephalic parapagus twins, usually called conjoined twins, who have one body and two heads. This will be followed by some considerations related to a clinical case of mother–child symbiosis. Watching the videos of conjoined twins is a good opportunity to put forward some theoretical clinical hypotheses around the subjectivation process.

The video can be considered as the starting point to reflect upon to what extent the mind is free to represent differentiated states with the same environmental and/or internal stimulation. So the question is: is it possible to construct one's own subjectivity under the same genetic and environmental conditions?

By extrapolation, the psychoanalytic setting can be examined through the same scenario: two people, constantly and regularly interacting in a room, where moments were tending to fusionality, alternate with moments pushing towards differentiation. These intersubjective/interpsychic movements (Spagnolo, 2017) become evident in transference/countertransference and in changes in the patient's defences. Moreover, in the analytical setting, the First-Person Perspective (FPP) and the Second-Person Perspective (SPP) continuously and mutually modify each other, through poorly known unconscious interactions, but which can be detected by means of what Freud (1915e) calls: 'The derivatives of the unconscious'.

The dicephalic twins also highlight the problematic framing of the concept of selfhood (First-Person Perspective, Second-Person Perspective, ownership, sense of agency, belongingness, and mineness).

DOI: 10.4324/9781003221876-3

Video presentation: Conjoined twins

More information on https://www.youtube.com/watch?v=5WnkBIWGh HAhttps://www.youtube.com/watch?v=cbIPVo4XnLI

A. and B. are among the very few conjoined twins who survived at birth in the world. They were born in Minnesota. At the time of this video recording, they were 23 years old and already had a university degree.

When they were born, the doctors stated they would have a short life expectancy and could not be separated for fear of losing one of them, and/or fatally disabling one or both of them. They are a rare example (1/40000) of dicephalic twins surviving at birth. They are probably the result of a single fertilized egg that did not become totally separated. There is no agreement among geneticists on this point. This is the situation of their internal organs:

They have two hearts, two spinal cords joined at the pelvis, two oesophaguses and two stomachs, a liver and a single intestine with a single urinary and reproductive system, a single rib cage with four partially joined lungs, three kidneys, a partially shared nervous system, as well as a shared circulatory system. They have two upper limbs and two lower limbs (a third rudimentary limb has been removed), but their necks and heads are clearly separated.

A., the one on the right (https://www.youtube.com/watch?v=5WnkBIWGhHA), does not perceive anything of the left side of body, B., the one on the left, does not perceive anything of the right side of the body. Nevertheless, the twins are capable of writing, driving, playing, swimming, and much more.

They feature a perfect motor coordination that allows them to move in unison in space, but they do not necessarily perceive, for example, the urgency of sleeping or eating at the same time. A. and B. eat their food in different dishes, alternating in shifts and helping each other, but they do not have the same food tastes; sometimes they dress the two 'sides' of the body differently to bring out their different personalities.

They buy two tickets for a theatre show or for the bus and, on their birthday, they blow out their candles on different cakes. They read and write at the same time, each using her own limb.

Their parents never asked for their separation because they are aware they may lose of one of the two, or they would be seriously disabled without four arms and four legs. They encouraged their differentiation by treating them as separate individuals, even if merged in one body.

Joint bodies, joint minds?

The first question that occurs is: are they two different persons or one?

They show two distinct personalities and behave (and subjectively perceive themselves) as two distinct individuals. They share and coexist in the same body that is likely mapped (then monitored, stored, represented) in two different brain structures. The obvious answer would be: one body, two minds.

If we start from the assumption that the mind–body unit is essentially framed into one body and one mind, we should conclude that one body corresponds to a single mind, so the twins are actually a unit. This logical reasoning does not help us settle the issue of the subjectivity perceived by the twins and, in this case, it leads us to ask whether the development of consciousness is really an 'entirely private, first-person phenomenon' (Damasio, 1999). In fact, as in the case of these twins, when there is a single body, subjectivity too is supposed to have a single shared nucleus of mentalized activity and therefore not able to experience any subjectively perceived difference. Instead, these twins describe themselves as separate units with distinct subjectivities, even if their body limits cannot be distinguished (the distinction of which part of the body belongs to one and which belongs to the other is not possible in this case). For A. and B., the question is what the boundary of the Self is, since this is born as bodily Self or embedded Self. For example, when B. yawns or coughs, A. immediately uses her right hand to cover her sister's mouth. Whose gesture is this both in terms of sense of agency and of sense of ownership? (Gallagher, 2000, 2005).

Often the sisters say the same thing simultaneously or, as their father and friends say, one may ask the other: 'Have you thought what I thought?' And without adding anything else, they do the same thing.

If the First-Person Perspective, i.e. FPP, conveys the mental states associated with one's Self and not with the Other's, the FPP should be entirely private and never accessible to the Other, being completely intra-subjective. What has just been described seems to suggest that the twin's FPP may be shared. However, if it shared, the FPP is no longer private, nor first-person based. This questions the very notion of FPP.

We can reflect more on '*Leib*' and '*Körper*' to better understand the concepts of mineness, i.e. what my body is as distinguished from your body, and belongingness, i.e. the body that belongs to me rather than to you. We can add that it is not '*Körper*', with the limits of its body surface, that marks the boundaries of the Self, but it is '*Leib*', the lived body, that marks its differences. However, in this case, the twins seem to be two persons, namely, two Selves experiencing one and the same lived body. Consequently, our example challenges the lived body as a hallmark feature of consciousness and its first-personal givenness, i.e. mineness.

The Bodily Self

Let us go back to what philosophy and neuroscience experts say about the body and how it relates to the Self. The experience of the lived body may be considered as the first essential manifestation of the Bodily Self. In minimal terms, it is this experience (lived Body) that shapes mineness and belongingness and, also, the sense of ownership and agency. Here ownership means that I am experiencing my body (*Leib*) as my body and not as the body of another person. So, we can say that, in this way, the twins experience their lived body in terms of mineness and belongingness.

It seems that there is an immediate, pre-reflective experience of minimal self or 'mineness' as one voluntarily performs bodily movements (at least in non-pathological cases). A central aspect of this experience of mineness is the sense of agency such that I experience the movement as intended, initiated and controlled by me.

(Hohwy, 2007, p. 4)

The sense of agency (involving other neuronal circuits, such as the cortical areas responsible for motor activities) is related to what I experience while I am moving, that is the action and the movements are mine since they were triggered by me as the agent; the sense of agency is more difficult to distinguish in these twin sisters.

What is experienced by the single body of these twins is encoded in the same way by their two different brains and their respective structures. The brain's intrinsic or spontaneous activity encodes Self-specific information (subjective) of the past and future, so the difference in intrinsic activity allows for constructing the Self and, in this case, the subjectivity of these individuals, even if their internal (interoception) and external (exteroception) stimulus inputs are the same.

Different and interconnected states of the self are embedded in the intrinsic activity of the brain that predisposes the construction of subjectivity and consciousness [...] How are these different states of the Self linked to the intrapsychic structure of individuals? Since the brain's intrinsic activity can be characterized by an individualized time-space structure, we suppose that all contents (whether affective, cognitive, social or sensorimotor) and their underlying extrinsic activity must first and foremost be integrated within the brain's spontaneous (internal) activity. The degree and the way the contents and their activities are integrated into the brain's spontaneous activity determine how we perceive them and hence how we experience them, i.e. our subjective or self-conscious experience of reality.

(Scalabrini et al., 2018, pp. 4–5)

The various sensory stimuli are, for instance, integrated in the spontaneous or intrinsic activity. This is how the stimuli from the different sensory modalities are integrated.

Multisensory integration

Multisensory Integration (Talsma, 2015) promotes the development of a new representational product through a neural process in which single or multiple stimuli are integrated and recombined. While it is generated, this product is in turn combined with other sources of information (for example, memory, attention, logical-mathematical reasoning, emotional-affective system) and then reinterpreted in the light of this long process. Multisensory integration allows reinterpreting and recombining the initial stimuli through feedback or recurrent loops. For example, Talsma writes:

> The general idea is that these recurrent feedback projections can send biasing signals to the perceptual brain areas. The feedback signals can then induce an increase in sensitivity in neurons responsive to the attended feature, while simultaneously causing a decrease in sensitivity of neurons not responsive to the attended feature.
>
> (Talsma, 2015, p. 5)

In a nutshell, in the case of these twins, a single body can serve two minds in different ways. The same intero- and exteroceptive inputs from the environment and their single shared body are processed and integrated within their two brains' intrinsic or spontaneous activities in different and thus individual ways. Even if they are exposed to the same intero- or exteroceptive stimuli, they will process them differently and thus perceive them in an individually specific and henceforth subjective way. The ascription of subjectivity and individuality cannot be traced to their body, namely, their lived body, but ultimately to the different intrinsic activities in their brains.

Let us imagine the reverse scenario, one brain with two bodies rather than two brains with one body. In that case, we would assume that these subjects perceive the different interoceptive inputs from their bodies in (more or less) the same way as they are processed by their single brain with the same spontaneous activity. That is exactly the opposite of the current scenario, where the same interoceptive input is perceived in two different ways as related to two different spontaneous or intrinsic activities of their respective brains.

We can now see that both scenarios, one brain with two bodies and two brains with one body, are just extremes of what happens in the 'normal' case, two brains and two bodies. If our hypothesis is right and if two brains and two bodies closely converge and do not differentiate from each other in their development, it is possible to have a scenario more or less similar to the one of our fictitious cases, i.e. one brain with two bodies.

But what happens when two bodies and two minds become so wrapped up during their development that they cannot see any differentiation?

BX clinical case: No movement, no change

This is the case of BX, diagnosed as a case of 'elective mutism' at the age of three.

BX is a beautiful girl, a miniature Barbie who observes and scrutinizes the world without ever uttering a word. She is six years old and she has all the typical behaviours of her age; she has no apparent developmental impairment. She cannot be given (verbal or performance) tests because she does not respond and performs few actions on demand. She does not avoid looking at other people; indeed, she stares at everyone in a challenging way. She does not have any problems in joining a group: she easily follows the group and does exactly what the group does or what the group is requested. She never talks to any of her peers or teachers: she does exactly what they do; that is, she is learning to imitate, copy, and replicate.

When she is with her family, she speaks to her parents, to her grandmother (not to her grandfather), and to her two younger siblings (one sister and one brother). She adequately interacts with all of them. It soon becomes evident that she expresses and conveys her mother's thoughts and intentions. However, her very beautiful mother has a severe physical gait impairment. Her daughter looks very much like her, but with no physical disability and she grows up healthy, beautiful, and thin like a little model. This is the way BX feels and perceives herself. She continuously and obsessively draws beautiful Barbie-girls saying, 'It's me'. When she speaks about herself, she uses the I pronoun, but to any direct request she answers: 'I don't know, let's ask Mum'; or 'Mum says that' without ever expressing a subjective thought of her own. At the age of 5, she starts a psychoanalytic psychotherapy (psychotherapist A) with three sessions per week and her parents join a parent training programme with the same therapist, but with a separate monthly session. In eight years of therapy, BX never says a single word to psychotherapist A.

In primary school, she is able to learn like everybody else, but she does not communicate in any way (not even through written expression). She was able to read and write regularly, do her homework, make calculations, but she did not respond by speaking or writing to anyone.

In a few words: only direct communication was impaired.

BX continues to be investigated and monitored. Some specialists diagnose her as autistic, others as a case of early-onset schizophrenia, but BX has the same skills as her peers (she plays, works, eats, and carries out all her daily routines independently), but she never speaks. She only speaks to five people and from the age of 7 to six people, including one of the authors of this book, who came into her life as a relational support to dissolve the symbiosis with her mother. This means that since she was 7 years old, BX has had two psychotherapists: one (psychotherapist A) treating her and her parents with psychoanalytic clinical sessions, and another one (psychotherapist B) treating her at home.

After years of monitoring, the diagnosis was elective mutism in psychosis.

When psychotherapist B met her at home for the first time, she was exactly as she had been described by psychotherapist A; psychotherapist B suddenly recognizes the family dynamics illustrated by psychotherapist A; BX welcomes her, as her mum's friend, and speaks to her immediately.

Within the family, she acts like a normal child, cheerful, witty, and lively. Her mother behaves in the same way: she is happy, lively, witty, and willingly accepts all the (psychotherapist's) proposals.

Psychotherapist B's diary, three decades ago

We start working, acting on daily activities, on the recognition of the Other as separate. I introduce the proper use of 'I', 'We', and 'Other', through a real reference to people or the use of objects, but it is difficult for her to acquire the 'I think' concept. It is Mum who thinks; it is Mum who says; it is Mum who chooses; if Mum does not choose, BX switches off, like a chargeless robot. The development of a complacent Self (with or without the verbal function depending on the situation) continues in parallel with a 'void within' where the structure of the mind and of its contents belongs to the Other. The body too belongs to the Other. BX's body is experienced by the mother–child couple as a single body, included in the mother's body. Her body is as an appendage of her mother's body, as the functioning part of her mother's body that cannot be separated. Two physically speaking bodies, but one of the two already has a structured mental form, while the other one does not have its own mental form, but a beautiful physical form that grows and develops as the mother sees it.

Breaking this equilibrium is difficult for me as a young psychotherapist. However, in almost four years of work, I try to promote BX's own dimensions (by using space in a different way, exploring places other than home and school, and by timing her life away from her mother's schedule). Since I am the only person not belonging to the family with whom she speaks, I have become the mediator between her and the external world: in the presence of others, BX listens and whispers to me the questions or the answers to provide. Sometimes, I deliberately make a mistake in reporting her words and she sensationally says: 'No, wait, I tell you better'.

In this way, she can experience the sound of her voice in the presence of the other and above all she can calmly experience the reaction of the other.

The first setting: Remembering the slow ticking of time

My home support role (4/5 times a week), with its more flexible setting (compared to the psychoanalytic one with tighter rules), promotes her ability to choose and decide. We can go out and wander around the neigh-bourhood, study together, go shopping, play with her little brothers, according to her likings and proposals. I use all these opportunities to broaden her knowledge of the world, introducing other perspectives beyond her mother's. Her obstinate mutism, at school and in therapy, does not help the development of evolved social skills mediated by verbal production. On the contrary, our freedom to move in different spaces from the home-school-setting therapy and our mutual and abundant verbal production allow her to have her point of view, different from her mother's. This exploration of the world enables me to extensively work on:

—non-intrusion, that is, no introduction of my point of view in place of her mother's;
—repeated changes of scenarios and choreographies to loosen the rigidity of her thought and encourage her adaptation to new things;
—different relational styles, not dictated by the same dysfunctional rules that she knows well and acts upon;
—dismantling complacency, which produces the coartation of the structure of her Self by binding it to the absence of changes.

In fact, her interactive style may be encapsulated in a few words: if nothing changes, everything remains the same, and the differences are cancelled. Uttering no words with the rest of the world paves the way to the elimination of change. Her complacency allows her to adhere to her maternal world, cutting away the vital branches that sprout through new experiences and reach out luxuriant (given her young age) to the world.

This is the sense of my support role that 'acts' in the real world to 'enrich' the inner world with a concrete reality capable of including the 'Other external to the Self'. In this sense, broadening the interactive range means widening the relational sphere, which means including new objects in the maps of affective relations. But if affects are not trans-formed, that is, if the affective investment on new objects does not take place, what kind of Self will BX develop over time? When I leave her for concomitant commitments that do not allow me to support her any fur-ther, she is about to enter middle school (11 years old).

I learned later (from psychotherapist A) that, when she was about 13 years old, she began to talk to everyone at school but not to her. She ended her psychoanalysis at 13 years of age without having ever uttered a word with her.

At the end of the parent training, the parents gifted psychotherapist A a table clock featuring these words: 'Remembering the slow ticking of time'.

We can add something more about this patient's speech: the quality (morphosyntax, content, prosody, etc.) was perfect and coherent. Usually she did not act like her mother (direct mirroring), but like her mother's beautiful object (Barbie doll) and she dressed up and behaved and spoke like a Barbie doll. Both BX and her mother were happy acting, thinking, and performing by attunement. The issue was who was the subject of all that. At that time, BX was not aware of all this. She acted as if the Other did not exist: if I do not take a different perspective from the Other, the Other's world and mine coincide. This is the core of any symbiosis.

Temporospatial dynamics

What is going on here? We above pointed out the central role of the brain's spontaneous activity and multisensory integration in shaping our subjective experience, i.e. the Self and consciousness. The spontaneous activity displays an intrinsic dynamic in time and space, referred to as temporospatial dynamics. Compare that to the ocean. You can see small fast waves and big slow waves occurring in variable time intervals and different spatial extensions; the ocean displays its intrinsic temporospatial dynamics. However, it is not purely intrinsic, as it is strongly shaped by the environmental context, that is the wind. So, the environmental context shapes the temporospatial dynamics of the ocean.

Now imagine several surfers try to ride the waves. The temporospatial dynamics of the waves may smash them against one another, or they may surf in parallel, mirroring the others. This process is similar to multisensory integration: the waves integrate and link the various surfers together like the brain's spontaneous activity integrates the different sensory inputs (multisensory integration).

This is exactly what happens in our clinical case. The mother signifies the environmental context where she shapes her daughter's mind like the wind, albeit to an abnormally strong degree; in turn, this shapes her brain's spontaneous activity (Northoff & Mushiake, 2019). This abnormally strong shaping may be due to either an abnormally strong and invasive mother or, alternatively, to an abnormally weak spontaneous activity in the daughter's brain, whose intrinsic dynamics is easily prone to be taken over, and to be completely shaped by the temporospatial dynamics of the mother's brain (through her behaviour).

Consequently, the daughter integrates the various sensory inputs always in reference to her mother, meaning her mother's input shapes any subsequent multisensory inputs and integration even from sources outside her mother. The daughter thus seems to remain unable to develop her own 'baseline' or default, that serves as a reference for any subsequent stimulus processing, including multisensory integration. Instead, the daughter's 'baseline' or default, is that of her mother: that is why the daughter perceives and acts in the world through her mother, whereas outside her mother's realm, she remains unable even to speak and communicate with others. Her mother thus provides the substitute of her own individual 'baseline' or default that is lacking in the daughter.

Psychotherapist B's diary, three decades later

I am contacted by BX's family members through one of my social media profiles and they ask me for an appointment. I had met BX last time 30 years earlier and I am very excited to receive her. She is accompanied by her whole family and they are as excited as me. We all have changed, transformed by age, with the signs of time printed on our faces and bodies; but we are still recognizable, except for BX. She is unrecognizable. She is a stout woman of over 40 years of age, with a stern and glum expression on her face. Even if she is moved to see me, something in her eyes conveys her suffering from a long illness. She immediately speaks to me, asking me about the places we used to visit in the past and of which I can hardly remember anything. She does not wait for the answer; she repeats the same question several times. Everyone tells me about her past years, about school, about her social retrenchment because she could not fit in any context, about the various antipsychotic medicines prescribed over time. BX's family has always managed her without any support, but now that she shows sudden mood changes, irritability, outbursts of anger, they believe that the only one who can intervene is me, since she has always spoken with me.

BX agrees to come to see me and we start a support psychotherapy once a week.

My sessions with BX are a paralyzing immersion in the past: BX does not describe her past to me. She lives in the past, in the period that we shared and from which she has never moved forward. She listens to the same music, watches the same cartoons, searches for the same places, and would like to wear the same clothes. Every discrepancy from this reality generates irrepressible outbursts of anger. BX is still able to tell/talk about herself. If she is invited to talk about herself, she can describe her daily routine; her changed body and the many things that she has done in these years. But if she is left to speak spontaneously, she talks exactly as if she was 7 or 10 years old.

She asks me about some details (the lyrics of a song, the corner shop, the things said or done together); I cannot add much to these because my memories have faded. She remembers exactly every single detail and is baffled because I 'have not remained still at the time she was eight years old'. She gets angry if I introduce a time that is different from the one she lives in.

I slowly learn to use concrete events, her and my displacements, the succession of seasons and our pauses, as elements able to introduce the objective dimension of time, next to her subjective time dimension.

The recognition of a differentiated Self

First of all, we establish that she must live with her window blinders open and follow the circadian rhythm; she must leave the house with some family member (she never goes out alone, her parents are afraid when they think she can do something by herself or with a non-family member, thus undermining any further development of her social interactions); she must interact by herself with the people she meets; she must autonomously manage her daily routine.

All this is accepted, monitored, and gently promoted by her parents. BX resists.

She would like to stay at home in the dark, without interacting with anyone or even meeting her neighbours in front of the elevator. She would like the world to become suddenly uninhabited, except for the only eight people with whom she speaks, so as to be able to leave the house. We work on this bizarre idea of the world populated by eight people and then on the persecutory experience linked to the encounter with 'the Other'. More broadly, we work on the recognition of a differentiated Self and therefore on her exit from the reassuring symbiosis in which the Other does not exist. This allows us to very slowly revisit these 30 long years: she talks about school and the discomfort to talk to all the other people. She explains to me her adolescence when she understood she was different and not amenable to be integrated; so gradually she learned to observe and hold inside. She never expressed an opinion; that of her Mum and Dad was enough.

The introduction in the session of the possibility that I may have a different idea with respect to her parents is fraught with obstacles and she becomes very irritated. My non-alignment with the status quo ante makes her angry and she often insults me or cries. She would have liked me to meet her at home, as in the past. She would have preferred that I had not married, that I had no children or a profession, and that the places of the past still existed so as to explore them together.

Her disappointment allows me to achieve two goals: to allow her to adapt to the current reality, where time has elapsed and spaces have changed, and to identify the traits of her disadaptive functioning and show them to her.

During the session, she reacts with anger and protests against the introduction of the objective dimension of time, while at home she obsessively reiterates her rituals of a shared routine and isolation (locked in her room to write, draw, and colour the same things linked to the past). Everything takes place extremely slowly. For me, 30 years is a long time, while for her, it is negligible because she has just moved only a little further than she was before.

The passage of time

Usually, we all have landmarks through which we measure the passage of time. BX has no landmarks. Even the major surgical operations she underwent over the years to treat some diseases seem to be placed in an indefinite time frame, neither objective nor subjective. If I intervene on this point she replies: '*I don't want to be here with you, I want to be in x, to see the shop y, which is next to z ...*'—and builds exactly the historical map of the past. She is able to repeat the same thing over and over again. It seems that time does not move with her.

During these occasional meetings I have with her parents, I understand that she feels very angry against the rest of the world that has evolved while she has remained a child.

We work on this and her answer is always the same: '*Why do (human beings) exist? If they did not exist, everything would be still*'. If the Other was not a reference outside of her, the space–time of the Self would not exist. For this reason, I do not work on her internal reality where she is always the little girl, her mother's appendage.

After, grasping this dimension full of 'inanimate objects', I introduce our body dimension in today's reality, which is the 'here and now' of our life. I propose she checks the places of the past: the ones that still exist and those that have changed, adding 'when, why, how' to that checklist. The idea is to match the memory traces displayed on the maps that she draws every day with those new updated maps. So, her internal maps, built on symbiosis, and which hardly convey a sense of subjective belonging, are reconstructed in the places previously visited and now transformed by time. At the beginning, she complains and is determined to describe the details of the places of the past, but gradually she adds a new map (for example, how that place has changed over time), thus introducing some landmarks as follows:

This place belongs to the time when my grandmother was alive, do you remember her? When we lived there in via ... there was this shop; then we moved to our new home to... near the sea ...

It is a new space map, related to the places visited, but now it has a 'before and an after time' frame that has transformed it. In this frame, life appears. People and circumstances enliven this frame.

One day, she decides to go and see these places and describes them to me in their current state. She hangs out with her sister, moving from one place to another, checking out the changes.

Since I have never seen them (the places we used to visit together), we cannot share the same perspective, i.e. the same maps. I cannot share her updating through a perfect attunement. So, I can point out how much this belongs to her and not to me. I stress, in the 'here and now' of the session, this concept: what she is telling me is not impersonal; it does not belong to everyone. Those are her maps, built up in the time spent together in the past and now revisited by our new time 'here'.

By concretely revisiting these places of the past and re-discovering the many events that have occurred over time, I can identify, and show her, what belongs to me, for example, the area around my studio she never saw before these new sessions. She allows her to place me in a different reality (the present, not the past) that cannot be shared. So, she asks her sister to accompany her over the weekend to visit the area around my studio, to map a chart of my places. In this way, she starts to place me outside of her space–time, and this gives her the dimension of the Other as different from herself.

This new distribution of space and time is a key point of our therapy. For instance, she begins to be aware that the time elapsed has been different for both of us, because I was not in a symbiosis, where there is no exchange, no evolution. Hence, she realizes that I have been out of this symbiosis. Consequently, this gets her very angry and she says:

You have children, you have other patients, and you are busy over the weekend; instead of sitting at your desk waiting for me.

I do not accept the stillness in which she confines me and sometimes, when she is pressuring me with questions about my weekend, I vaguely say that: I have been at a conference, at the beach, on the mountains, at home. My answers are, indeed, not real; they actualize my proposal to undermine her purpose to freeze my time.

The private space of the Self

After three very long years, I see an opening in the denial of the existence of the Other and therefore an opening towards her differentiation. It is a small private space of the Self where BX begins to experiment with new possibilities in her life. She listens to new music without telling anyone; the cartoons she watches on TV are different from the ones in the past; she reads, but not the usual fairy tales. She asks to be taken to go shopping, and she wants to personally deal with the shop assistants and to choose her clothes. Later, I see her body change; she has lost weight, she dresses up with care and attention, she looks like a woman over 40 years of age. For the first time in her life, she goes to the cinema.

This new opening leads her to painfully realize the isolation in which she has lived, unleashing her intentions to revenge against all those who have not understood her.

So, this is the beginning of a period in which she is truly angry with her past and with all the people she has met and whom she now wants to erase. She becomes obsessed with all the encounters she has made and that she can no longer change. She has sudden fits of anger towards her parents, who are afraid of her. By analyzing together what happens to her in those moments of rage she adds:

I feel crazy because if my past had been different, I'd be another BX now.

This is how the most difficult part of our work starts: she has to accept change, the passage of time, what she is now, which means to abandon the past with all her memories and accept new openings.

One day, she asks me when we would stop seeing each other. I do not have a date to give her, but she wants it and insists on having it. She claims:

I must know when we would leave each other, because I can continue to come only for some more time. I am a grown-up woman and not a child any longer.

I do not know what to say to her, so she adds: *I'll come until you retire, do you agree with me?* and I answer: *In more than twenty years, I think,* she replies: *Of course, just twenty more years and then we break up.*

I understand that time is not still for this woman/girl/child, but it flows so slowly that 20 years can be enclosed in a few moments. I think back to the clock given by her parents to psychotherapist A, 30 years earlier. During the next session with her parents, I talk to them about this detail. Much to my surprise, they reveal that it has always been difficult to communicate with their daughter, because she takes a very long time to process the answer: usually weeks.

What if her slow mental functioning has been one of the causes of the retarded growth and maturation of the structure of the Self?

Considerations on psychopathology and treatment

What is the diagnosis of this patient? We may assume it is an extreme form of autism characterized by an extremely long-lasting and a restricted space in her subjective inner consciousness that is supposedly linked to abnormal temporospatial patterns in her brain's spontaneous activity. So, her psychopathological features, including her abnormal behaviour, may be the result of her abnormal inner time and space experience. In fact, we do not believe it is a case of schizophrenia or psychosis a deux characterized by the fragmentation of the inner time consciousness, but rather a case with an abnormally long-lasting timescale as in autism.

The latest studies on neurodevelopmental disorders, including autism, take into account many neurobiological parameters.

Singletary (2015) points to maladaptive plasticity as one of the mechanisms that produce the severity of the disorder if no timely intervention is undertaken. He assumes that the child, due to its neurobiological vulnerability, experiences its inability to interact with the environment, i.e. social isolation and social deprivation, and that this causes stress and an allostatic load. It is the physical and psychological overload of the response to be given to the environment that can damage the body. The neurobiological and psychological factors involved in the development of symptoms interact in a non-linear way through this allostatic overload that leads to maladaptive coping and maladaptive neuroplasticity. Through an early psychodynamic approach designed to include the care environment and to promote social integration and stress reduction, it is possible to curb maladaptive neuroplasticity and to promote adaptive neuroplasticity.

In the transition from childhood to adult life, our patient was able to cope with many developmental steps through the first interventions that promoted her adaptive coping. However, coping (the ability to cope with situations) was not sufficient for her to manage social skills. The neurobiological vulnerability in space and time processing prevented its further evolution. This well described by Watanabe et al. (2019), in one of their research studies:

> We found that in adults with ASD, the intrinsic timescale was significantly shorter in the bilateral postcentral gyri and right inferior occipital gyrus, and longer in the right caudate. The shorter intrinsic timescale in these primary sensory/visual areas in autism was correlated with the overall severity of autism. The longer intrinsic timescale in the caudate in autism was associated with the severity of repetitive, restricted behaviours.
>
> (p. 9)

The studies on brain 'connectivity' have started a wide debate about the neurotypical organization of some psychopathologies. Hull et al. (2017) report that:

> Ongoing debate exists within the resting-state functional MRI (fMRI) literature over how intrinsic connectivity is altered in the autistic brain, with reports of general overconnectivity, under-connectivity, and/or a combination of both. Classifying autism using brain connectivity is complicated by the heterogeneous nature of the condition, allowing for the possibility of widely variable connectivity patterns among individuals with the disorder.
>
> (Hull et al., 2017, p. 1)

This debate is the framework of the studies on 'dysperception' (Ouss & Guénolé, 2016), which can describe the impairment of relational skills in autism. There are many more studies in the literature, but we want to go back to the atypical neurodevelopment model, which highlights that psychopathologies may have different outcomes depending on the treatment and on its timing; consequently, due to neuroplasticity modelling, the diagnosis can range between various extremes.

After some many decades, and different types of treatment (including drugs), we can say that BX's stable pathological (or neuro-atypical) nucleus can be detected in her slow timescale and in her tendency to social isolation (non-recognition of the Other).

We can also describe all this in terms of 'salience':

> The abnormal predominance of slow frequency power in SN may predispose ASD subjects to rely on different temporal patterns when processing the salience of environmental events and integrating exteroceptive and interoceptive stimuli. This is well in accordance with clinical practice, which reported that ASD patients are rather inflexible in their behaviour. For instance, they show difficulties when asked to quickly answer to unexpected events or new situations (Hodgson et al., 2016), they are extremely slow in adapting to variations of their daily routine (South et al., 2005) and show qualitative alterations in perception of both time flow and time structure (Vogel et al., 2018).
>
> (Damiani et al., 2019, p. 6)

What does a salient stimulus mean from the point of view of the organization of a brain circuit? It means that the incoming stimulus goes through preferential pathways and it is difficult to make it switch to other pathways. In this way, the objective investments (therefore on the environment and the caregiver) follow the original imprinting, in our case linked to the structure of her mother's Self.

What else does this clinical case tell us to better describe this poor transformability?

The case nicely illustrates that her subjective time and space is altered. The temporospatial dynamics of our brain's spontaneous activity shapes our mental states, the way we experience ourselves and others in time and space. We have a virtual 3D time–space structure in our consciousness that is part of multisensory integration; this is experienced as inner time and space consciousness which is very much altered in our case. Her subjective timescale is no longer dynamic but static; it is almost frozen at the time of her childhood when it first developed, as in close interaction with her mother. The duration of her subjective timescale is extremely long, which results in the extremely slow nature of her subjective experience and of her behaviour, including her cognition. Such an extremely long-lasting timescale prevents her from changing, accommodating, and updating, her subjective time consciousness according to the changing environment; this is a typical feature of autism, where patients are extremely slow relative to the faster environment.

So, the first psychopathological feature is the extremely long duration of her inner time consciousness; we assume that is due to the abnormal predominance of the slow frequencies with their long cycle in her brain's spontaneous activity (Damiani et al., 2019). This abnormally long duration explains her static perception and cognition as well as her memory of the past; she lives in the past because she is not able to switch to a shorter duration of her inner time consciousness.

The second psychopathological feature is her abnormally restricted subjective space. Her subjective space is limited to the one in which she grew up, that is, her childhood space. Any deviation from that space cannot be integrated since her subjective space remains too restricted and static and related to her long-lasting timescale. Again, since we assume that time and space are the 'common currency' of neuronal and mental activity (Northoff et al., 2019), we suggest that the abnormal spatial restriction in terms of her behaviour and consciousness can be traced to her brain's spontaneous activity and how it constructs her own inner space (Huang et al., 2016).

Her last psychotherapy worked on the change of space–time landmarks, introducing the reality of the relationship with the therapist in the intersubjective exchange. Since this relationship is: strongly 'affective' (therefore able to promote new investments); long-lasting (from the past to the present and projected to the future, therefore able to promote memory consolidation and reconsolidation); outside the familiar scheme (i.e. placed in a physical and mental space outside the usual space); it has been able to nourish her Self with new affective and cognitive resources, thus promoting small changes; however, in which direction? We can say towards autonomy, that is, the acquisition of some more adaptive social skills, even if not extremely performative.

References

Damasio, A. (1999). *The feeling of what happens.* New York: Harcourt, Brace.

Damiani, S., Scalabrini, A., Gomez-Pilarc, J., Brondinoa, N., & Northoff, G. (2019). Increased scale-free dynamics in salience network in adult high-functioning autism. *Neuroimage: Clinical,* 21: 1–10.

Freud, S. (1915e). *The unconscious. S.E.,* 14:159–204. London: Hogarth.

Gallagher, S. (2000). Philosophical conceptions of the self: implications for cognitive science. *Trends in Cognitive Science,* 4(1):14–21.

Gallagher, S. (2005). *How the body shapes the mind.* Oxford: Oxford University Press.

Hodgson, A. R., Freeston, M. H., Honey, E., Rodgers, J. (2016). Facing the unknown: Intolerance of uncertainty in children with autism spectrum disorder. *Journal of Autism and Developmental Disorders,* 30(2):336–344.

Hohwy, J. (2007). The sense of self in the phenomenology of agency and perception. *Psyche,* 13(1): 1–20.

Huang, Z., Obara, N., Davis, H. H., Pokorny, J., & Northoff, G. (2016). The temporal structure of resting-state brain activity in the medial prefrontal cortex predicts self-consciousness. *Neuropsychologia,* 82:161–170.

Hull, J.V., Jacokes, Z.J., Torgerson, C.M., Irimia, A., & Van Horn, J.D. (2017). Resting-state functional connectivity in autism spectrum disorders: A review. *Frontiers Psychiatry,* 7(205):1–17.

Northoff, G., Wainio-Theberge, S., & Evers, K. (2019). Is temporo-spatial dynamics the 'common currency' of brain and mind? In quest of 'spatiotemporal neuroscience'. *Physics of Life Reviews*, 2019. https://doi.org/10.1016/j.plrev.2019.05.002 [Epub ahead of print].

Northoff, G., & Mushiake, H. (2019). Why context matters? Divisive normalization and canonical microcircuits in psychiatric disorders. *Neuroscience Research*, 2019. https://doi.org/10.1016/j.neures.2019.10.002 [Epub ahead of print].

Ouss, L., & Guénolé, F. (2016). Deprivation, dysperception, or dyssynchrony? A discussion of Singletary's integrative model of autism spectrum disorder. Commentary on 'An integrative model of autism spectrum disorder: ASD as a neurobiological disorder of experienced environmental deprivation, early life stress, and allostatic overload' by William M. Singletary, MD. *Neuropsychoanalysis*, 18(1): 15–18.

Scalabrini, A., Mucci, C., & Northoff, G. (2018). Is Our Self Related to Personality? A Neuropsychodynamic Model. *Frontiers in Human Neuroscience*, 12(346):1–9.

Singletary, W.M. (2015). An integrative model of autism spectrum disorder: ASD as a neurobiological disorder of experienced environmental deprivation, early life stress and allostatic overload. *Neuropsychoanalysis*, 17(2):81–119.

South, M., Ozonoff, S., McMahon, W. M. (2005). Repetitive behavior profiles in Aspergersyndrome and high-functioning autism. *Journal Autism Developmental Disorders*, 35:145–158.

Spagnolo, R. (2017). An unexpected pathway for interpsychic exchange: Music in the analysis of young adult. In B. N. Seitler & K. S. Kleinman (Eds), *Essays from cradle to couch* (pp. 341–357). Astoria: IP Books.

Talsma, D. (2015). Predictive coding and multisensory integration: an attentional account of the multisensory mind. *Frontiers in Integrative Neuroscience*, 9(19):1–13.

Watanabe, T., Rees, G., & Masuda, N. (2019). Atypical intrinsic neural timescale in autism. *eLife*, 8:1–18.

Vogel, D., Falter-Wagner, C. M., Schoofs, T., Kramer, K., Kupke, C., Vogeley, K. (2018). Interrupted time experience in autism spectrum disorder: empirical evidence from content analysis. *Journal Autism Developmental Disorders*, 49:22–33.

Chapter 3

The Self and the world

The complexity of the Self

One of the features of psychoanalysis is to be in line with the current historical and social reality through the stories of patients. Their narratives bring contemporary issues into the analysis room, such as the transformations brought about by the global use of the internet in the last two decades of the last century.

As of the 1980s,[1] patients bring with them in the analytical sessions the digital revolution and its new and evolving forms of communication, including the use of social networks (SNs).

Social networks deploy their power within the network, called the web, which is considered as a virtual reality system (cyberspace);[2] due to its intrinsic characteristics, this space makes it possible to have a prevailing '*sine-corpo*' relational mode, which may lead to pathological dependence behaviours called '*sine-substantia*'.

In this '*sine-substantia*' reality, subjects may create numerous 'variants of their Self', which simultaneously interact with many other individuals (other variants), without the limits imposed from the body on distinctive personification. 'Interactive identities are consciously constructed and jettisoned into cyberspace; these identities can be shaped to allow any fantasied aspect of the Self to come alive' (Sand, 2007, p. 84).

This change ('*sine-corpo*' relational multiplicity) experienced 'online' has major repercussions on 'offline' life and it forces us to rethink the meaning of some dualities, such as presence–absence, real–unreal, contact–relation, public–private.

Considerations on cyberspace

Human relations have been redesigned and redefined since the advent of cyberspace. Digital natives are born and raised among mobile phones, robotic toys, and videogames, which are operated using icons, and they no longer need to read to be able to utilize them. The virtual world cannot be considered as something parallel to the reality of objects, i.e. as something that multiplies the

DOI: 10.4324/9781003221876-4

real Self, but as a phenomenon that is embedded in everyday life. As a result, now the development of the Self is also fed by cyberspace and by its means of communication which contribute to its functional scaffolding on a par with affects, emotions, and cognition. The relationships built within and through cyberspace (*sine-substantia* relations) are biographically relevant and cannot be distinguished from '*cum-substantia*' relations. In order to better understand the quality of these Self–Object or Self–Other relations, we must look at digital natives in whom this process is completely spontaneous and authentic. In fact, cyberspace is as real as the reality of material 'objects' for them. Digital natives are individuals *who can easily utilize 'non-real objects'* and relate to them as if they were concrete objects. In this meaning of 'real', the Self–Other relationship (two different relational poles as synonyms of intersubjectivity) expands to become a Self–world relationship. In this Self–world relationship, the boundaries of the Self and of the Other are blurred, so the concept of intersubjectivity loses its bi-univocal relational meaning.

The Self is immersed in this material or immaterial reality that is continuously shaping and permeating it; it is a Self–Other with a window always open onto the world–community. 'Always on' (always connected) means a window always open onto the surrounding environment, and onto the globalized and/or spatially distant environment, which are close timewise. This is the reality on the internet: time and space collapse into a micellar present where the dichotomies such as local–global, near–far, present–absent, lose their ability to provide direction as knowledge carriers, i.e. mutual flows of metaknowledge between the Self and the World built on intersubjectivity. The way in which the web is utilized enables the user to hold a double simultaneous position, as a subject here and now, but also an object, as a node of the system; this defines (double face relationship) the eccentric nature of the subject on the network (being the Self and the Other at the same time), which completely demolishes the concept of intersubjectivity. We may say that the web brings about the 'One, No One and One Hundred Thousand' by Pirandello (2016), without any responsibility and authenticity *vis-à-vis* the different aliases and, above all, without being oppressed by the constraints that space, time, and body impose on everyday life. By constantly using technology and keeping up with its accelerated pace to 'get' to the other, the individual is public by default, and private by effort (Hardey & Atkinson, 2018). The Other is not a subject (or an object) but simply an interface with the world (with a global reality).

Rosen writes:

> For centuries, the rich and the powerful documented their existence and their status through painted portraits. A marker of wealth and a bid for immortality, portraits offer intriguing hints about the daily life of their subjects—professions, ambitions, attitudes, and, most importantly, social standing [...] Today, our self-portraits are democratic and digital; they are

crafted from pixels rather than paints. On social networking websites like Myspace and Facebook, our modern self-portraits feature background music, carefully manipulated photographs, stream-of-consciousness musings, and lists of our hobbies and friends. They are interactive, inviting viewers not merely to look at, but also to respond to, the life portrayed online.

(Rosen, 2007, p. 15)

This continuous exposure to the other makes the notion of privacy and authenticity obsolete, as it has produced a shift from know thyself to show thyself (Rosen, 2007) and also supports the illusion of disembodiment. Among the many consequences of disembodiment and the absence of privacy and authenticity, these subjects can shape their body and adjust their own story with no continuity with their biography. Moreover, interpersonal relationships have become broader and more transparent, this expanding the concept of group into the concept of community.

Online, I argue, there is no group, and likely no individual in the traditional sense of them. The kind of reflective space that people call containment is provided by infinite access, rather than through the group process. The idea that knowing means uncovering something inchoate (and that the group incubates and contains this struggle) is replaced with a notion of freedom by accretion. Freedom for personal expression is a move toward ever-greater accessibility of objects via interface with others. One's object are not destroyed when others add to them or alter them, or even, cancel them: they morph. Structures—i.e. rules that delimit what is a self, what is a group, what is knowledge, etc.—morph accordingly.

(Hartman, 2012, p. 457)

The digital world is a three-dimensional if not multi-dimensional virtual world. The common time and space features of our reality are transposed in the 3D/multi-dimensional cyberspace. The cyberspace thus creates a virtual temporospatial reality within the real temporospatial reality, our daily life. The virtual and real world are different in their degree of time and space extension, but they share their time and space construction on a deeper and more fundamental level. Both these worlds are thus intrinsically temporospatial; they are a temporospatial space, albeit with different degrees of temporospatial extension. Their shared temporospatial space has a major impact on our brain's response and even more on future psychiatric psychotherapy.

The compulsive use of Facebook

Doctor, something unthinkable is happening to me. I have been spying on my ex on Facebook (Fb). At the beginning, I just used to read his posts. Then I started reading, wherever possible, the posts of his contacts and little by little I found myself looking into photos, dates, FB events, to closely check on him. He is always present in my life. I always know everything about him. He is more present now that we have broken up than when we were engaged. My life can be summed up in a few words: you are part of my reality, I know what you are doing moment after moment, I am there with you every moment, but I am not part of your reality.

CX is a young graduate belonging to the 'i generation' with good social skills; however, since her boyfriend left her (he simply disappeared for no good reason, according to her), she has started not to eat, to vomit every day, to isolate herself more and more, thus narrowing her field of interests down to one: following her ex-boyfriend on Fb with all his contacts, being careful not to be exposed.

She considers herself someone in between a geek[3] and nerd,[4] impossible to block, impossible to self-lock.

Since the first sessions, she has talked about this reality made of posts, photos, events, contacts, and exchanges through which she follows her former boyfriend, without ever meeting him, talking or writing to him. It is an obsession that fills her days and her mind and with which she fills and saturates our meetings. At the end of the three exploratory talks, when she asks anguished how she can get out of such a strong 'mental trip', she gets this answer:

In the meantime, let's ask ourselves what you feel you have left of yourself on Fb that perhaps you would like to recover, but that you cannot recover because you don't know where you left it (inside or outside of yourself), you don't know to whom it belongs (to you, to your boyfriend, to the reality of Fb). And maybe, you don't even know what you left and therefore what you have to leave behind.

The Fb material comes up during the session as a daily tale of events within the *sine-substantia* reality in which she is totally immersed. CX agrees to start psychoanalytic therapy; she feels this message belongs to her and can share it because, with a brief comment, the analyst has not denied the Fb reality in which she is immersed. The compulsive use of Fb responds to her personal need (which the patient understands even if she does not know what it is); she is also aware that the easy way in which she uses it to control her boyfriend actually lends itself to abuse.

We will find this case again in the clinical discussion.

This is another patient with a different situation; here is a short summary:

CY is a gentleman in his late 50s who separated from his wife a few months earlier. He wants to start an analysis because he no longer talks to his ex-wife, except during the weekly exchange of their children. After the separation, he found himself spying on her life on Fb. Now he knows everything about his ex-wife: where she goes, whom she meets, how she feels during the events posted on Fb. Every detail found on her wall or in her Fb contacts is used to trace her daily life. Fb is always active on her profile, and he watches it every single minute to avoid missing a single detail. Through their children, his former wife learns that she is constantly monitored by her former husband, so she blocks him.

CY is not a nerd; he does not know how to get around the ban and feels extremely anxious for having suddenly lost this daily contact with his ex-wife (with his ex-wife's Fb profile). For him, it is intolerable not to know anything about her anymore. One day, during the weekly exchange of their children, bursting with anger for not having access to the details of her life, he provokes a fight and beats her to death.

In the first case, the patient compulsively spied on her former boyfriend for more than six months after having started the psychotherapy; later, she managed to leave him to his no-longer-boyfriend fate. The psychoanalytic work through the defensive mechanisms underlying her control on Fb helped her give up that control. She managed to analyse her anguish of loss (of the boundaries of the Self and of the object) without the intermediation of Fb, facing her relationship with the community in the analysis.

In the second case, the subject was blocked on Fb and he was deprived of access to his former wife's reality, thus prematurely closing off the inter-psychic corridor (Spagnolo, 2017), which fed both the contact with his ex and the connection with the analytical space. In this way, the tangible reality of her absence abruptly materialized as a loss, generating an overwhelming feeling of anguish, and pushing him to become a murderer.

Temporospatial alignment

In these two cases, can we speak of Internet Abuse (IA) or Social Networks Addiction (SNs Addiction)? Or has the frequent and careless use of the medium (the internet) simply paved the way to control compulsion with all its consequences? What kind of transformation of the media-induced Self comes into the analysis?

Both examples show how the virtual reality of Fb has taken over the physical reality of the real world. Both subjects could easily switch between the real world and the virtual world, so how is this possible? We postulate that this switch between the two worlds is just a switch between two different temporospatial frames, that of the real world and the one of the virtual world (of Fb). What is important for the Self is to be embedded and aligned to its respective temporospatial context, which goes beyond the body and embodiment to the world itself. However, it is not the real world as such into which the Self wants to be embedded and align itself to maintain its stability; rather, it is the temporospatial features of their respective context, i.e. usually the real world to which the Self and its brain align to.

We can then speak of temporospatial alignment.

The interesting issue in these cases is that such temporospatial alignment is now shifted from the real to the virtual world; the latter and its temporospatial construction takes over the role of the real world. Now the Self no longer aligns to the real world because of the psychic pain related to the loss of the real partner. Now, not being able to cope with the loss of the partner, the Self of these subjects aims at regaining that partner in a virtual way, that is through the cyberworld, through Fb. So, the virtual partner replaces the real partner; psychodynamically, we can speak of defence mechanisms where the real partner is projected upon the virtual partner in the cyberworld. Instead of aligning itself to the temporospatial coordinates of the real world and the real partner, the Self now aligns itself to the temporospatial frame of the virtual cyberworld, of Fb, so as to regain or better preserve the partner at least in a virtual way and to maintain its stability. In this way, this escape from reality can be better conceived as the virtual temporospatial preservation of the partner, which is more or less the same but, in a way, more real than a purely mental escape where all the subject's imagination and dreams circle around his or her lost partner. Again, the mental escape is only slightly different, as it fundamentally shares with the escape from the real world and the virtual cyberworld the same temporospatial frame to which the Self aligns itself to remain stable, i.e. temporospatial alignment, albeit with different degrees of temporospatial extension in real, virtual, and mental worlds.

Internet addiction: Some considerations

Many of the studies on internet addictions come from Griffiths (1995, 2000), who identified six common elements in technological addictions (*sine-substantia*) and in drug addictions. In 1996, Young conducted a pilot study on more than 600 people to better describe the 'Internet Addiction Disorder' (IAD), a form of addiction resulting from the abuse of mass communication media (Young, 1996). This study produced an interesting finding: dependent subjects mainly use the web functions linked to interactive activities (social–relational use), while non-dependent people use the web to search for information (performative use).

In the following years, an increasing number of studies focused on how to describe internet addictions and how to classify them: Morahan-Martin (2008) wrote about the great alarm triggered by the abuse of the internet. Citing the results of many studies, the author highlighted that there was no general consensus on the term IAD to define a clinical entity in which there is no substance abuse. This addiction was defined with different terms such as internet addiction, compulsive use of the internet, pathological or problematic use of the internet. The author showed that these labels were actually different ways of conceptualizing this disorder. She proposed to use the term Internet Abuse, without identifying a specific pathology:

Those who are chronically lonely and those who are socially anxious share many characteristics, which may predispose them to develop IA. Both are apprehensive in approaching others, fearing negative evaluations and rejection. They tend to be self-preoccupied with their perceived social deficiencies, which leads them to be inhibited, reticent, and withdrawn in interpersonal situations and avoid social interactions.

(Morahan-Martin, 2008, pp. 52–53)

She suggested the term IAs (Internet Abuse Specific) for online sexual addictions (Meerkerk, et al., 2006) and games (massively multiplayer online role-playing games—MMORPGs), as also reported by Leménager et al. (2013), thus excluding the social networks from the IAs (Internet Abuse Specific) group.

According to Kuss and Griffiths (2011), there are very few studies specifically devoted to social media abuse and this type of abuse has to be included in the Cyber-Relationship Addictions (an addiction to online relationships by Young, 1999).

From a clinical psychologist's perspective, it may be plausible to speak specifically of 'Facebook Addiction Disorder' (or more generally 'SNS Addiction Disorder') because addiction criteria, such as neglect of personal life, mental preoccupation, escapism, mood modifying experiences, tolerance, and concealing the addictive behavior, appear to be present in some people who use SNSs excessively.

(Kuss & Griffiths, 2011, p. 3529)

At present, all the authors dealing with this subject criticize the extensive use of this label, given the large percentage of people (hundreds of millions) who utilize the SNs for social purposes such as, for example, acquiring and maintaining online and offline relations, as well as promoting their activities.

On the other hand, back in 1997, Lévy had already suggested that the Social Networks should be seen as a new form of 'collective intelligence' (Lévy, 1997). In 1984, Turkle opened a debate on psychoanalysis and web reality (games and chat rooms which promote the expression of multiple identities), and invited us to consider these new technologies as 'evocative objects' (Turkle, 1984, 1995, 2002) that force us to have a different vision of ourselves and of the world.

As an addition to Turkle's thoughts, Gabbard (2001) asked whether these new interactive identities, which develop in or through the web, might be used in the analysis and proposed a tight comparison between the transitional space and virtual reality. While Suler (2008) emphasized the need to integrate the split parts of the Self experienced online as separate from the rest of the offline life. Lemma (2010, 2015) expanded her reflections on the incorporeal nature of online relationships and suggested that the analysts should better focus on their patients' experience with these new technologies, since they may also serve a psychological development purpose and are not necessarily synonymous with psychopathology.

In conclusion, the current studies on specific samples of users provide conflicting data on the susceptibility of the massive users of Social Networks (Facebook in almost all research studies) to the onset of the compulsive behaviours and addictions, which may be classified as a well-defined pathological category (Blau, 2011; Gencer & Koc, 2012; Ryan et al., 2014; Chakraborty, 2016).

There is still an open question as to 'what' we are dealing with when we meet patients who compulsively and obsessively utilize the Social Networks, since this type of compulsion cannot be restricted to a psychopathological category of its own; in fact, it is at the crossroad of broad pathological categories (Rosen, 2011), and of various personality types (Kuss & Griffiths, 2011).[5]

Three perspectives: Online life, offline life, integration

Here we are talking about individuals who concretely know each other, who have been in contact, who have experienced a mutual bond for a period of their lives (Kaes, 2008), and then who got separated.

When this bond is broken, control compulsion sets in. Therefore, we may say that this type of compulsion is very different from the compulsive use of chat rooms, for example, since these rooms are completely anonymous, impersonal, and full of fake identities. In the case studies presented here, the users' identification coincides with their real identity.

In line with Walther (1996), and to his three levels of computer-mediated impersonal, interpersonal, and hyperpersonal communication (CMC), we may say that it is not only the impersonal elements of online relationships (which variously elicit regressive, split, idealized and narcissistic elements of the Self) that have a specific role in patients who cannot stop controlling their (ex) partner's profile, but also the interpersonal elements of their offline lives, that allow them to relive (and enliven) this online relationship without any possibility to integrate the separation. There is no separation because the other is never absent; the partner's continuous presence in the Fb cyberspace (constant uploading of personal information) may lead to a continuous libidinal reinvestment of the object, thus effectively preventing the ego from abandoning it and finalizing the mourning phase (Hartman, 2012).

The parting of the other from the personal relationship (through the subtraction of the psycho-physical elements previously provided to the bond) never result in an absence. In fact, Fb provides the (even minimal) hyperpersonal signals that intensify the interpersonal feedback and feed the relationship with the other by being 'always connected', thus effectively preventing the separation. In this way, the medium (social network) offers an important support to the structuring of defences and resistances no longer linked to the sensory elements that the body imposes on the physical relationship (Lemma, 2010), or even to the 'representation' of the absence of the other. In other words, *the interaction through Fb simultaneously takes away the body and the representation of the absence.*

We should therefore ask ourselves what kind of mourning of the loss is possible. Gibbs (2007) writes:

> Some individuals are essentially relating to themselves on the Internet/ computer, and might be described as narcissistic. Depressed persons seeking to avoid the risk of interpersonal loss may hope to do so by controlling the Other, and confining relationships to the virtual. Finally, individuals called herein 'schizoid' or 'paranoid' withdraw into the safety of an internal world, finding the world of the Other taxing, persecuting, or simply nonexistent. What ties all these individuals together is each patient's need to control the object on the Internet/computer, hoping to escape fears that overwhelmingly catastrophic affect would be associated with interaction not so controlled.
>
> (Gibbs, 2007, p. 11)

In order to escape from the anguish of the loss, the illusion of the bond with the other is perpetuated through a virtual contact in cyberspace. This contact, represented by the many contacts that form a network woven around thousands of profiles, generates endless possible stories in which to include the story of the controlled object, and keeps this bond alive. Within this 'multi-authored' and variously constructed story (from photographs, posts, music, and comments), it becomes easy to extract some elements to support the permanence of this bond. Infinite possible stories, therefore, narratives, not multiple selves acting in a differentiated way according to the objects to which they refer.

> No longer bound by the limitations of the body, one can interact online in a multiplicity of ways that offers an experience that is less available in real life, such as changing gender, race, age, etc. (Turkle, 1997). It is a paradoxical space, as a transitional space it may be more constrained because of the need for an ideational narrative in which actions must unfold; yet it is also a more flexible space, because the body doesn't limit the action.
>
> (Sand, 2007, p. 85)

What more does Fb offer with respect to real life? It offers the slight touch of omnipotence that reifies the presence of the other; that is, in the cases described, it reifies the encounter with the lost other. The subtraction of the body from the relationship does not alter the relationship itself, since Fb is a container of the life of the other, in which the other continues to live. To better understand this point, let us briefly look at the two clinical cases described.

Nebulization of the boundaries

In the first case, the patient had a strong desire to continue her relationship with her beloved partner. The possibility to get back to him through the Facebook reality, even if she was very distressed by her estrangement from this reality, allowed her to continue to love him (to love what he did), paying the price of a strong idealization of this reality and of the lives taking place there. The obsessive isolation into which she had plunged served to banish the elements that might disavow the separate reality of the other from her offline life.

We may say that the nebulization of the boundaries between the real life and the virtual reality, produced by the web culture, makes it possible to live in a community of friends (generation of friends, Schirmacher, 2007) sheltered from close dual bonds; at the same time, it also allows for the illusion of the bond with the beloved object through the connection with the many contacts created (contacts in terms of number of connected profiles and, above all, number of visits on the controlled profile, so number of likes).

The illusion of the existence of a bond is maintained by the constant presence of the other on the social network stage (if the other was not part of this network and was not an active promoter of his or her profile, there would be no illusion of belonging to the same system). This illusion that abruptly crumbles when a contact is banned.

As described in the second case: suddenly the banned subject is out of the scene, his link with the other is totally severed, triggering rampant separation anguish; and if his defences are not shifted onto the control of the social networks, the material reality of his separated body and its ability to act kicks in without any barrier to prevent him from acting.

In this sense, the contact with the other through this virtual interactive dimension protects against a contact/connection with catastrophic feelings of anguish and abandonment.

We can anticipate that, with the first patient, it was possible to mend the tear between her online and offline life, thus integrating the elements of the Self deposited online and bringing them back within the boundaries of her offline Self. By putting these omnipotent and controlling aspects of her Self on Facebook, the analytical relationship was able to explore (and reconstruct) the boundaries of the Self, thus shielding her from an early destructiveness that would have undermined the analytical work.

With the second patient, these protective elements did not have the time to develop, given the early and abrupt interruption of his link with the digital container (early means before working through these aspects in the analytical container); this led not only to acting, but to the discontinuation of the therapy.

We will now analyze the first clinical case, CX: we will briefly focus on the initial phase of treatment of her compulsive use of Fb and follow up the evolution of her psychotherapy until it unveils the patient's participation in a therapeutic community that was popular some years ago.

What psychiatrists describe as addiction is just a different way of stabilizing the Self. In this case, the Self is stabilized not through the alignment to the real world, but through the alignment to the virtual cyberworld. Alignment constitutes the relation and the relation stabilizes the Self; if the real world is too painful and absent in the mental life of a subject due to the loss of his or her partner, the Self aligns itself to the virtual cyberworld to regain its stabilization. So, what doctors call addiction is an attempt to stabilize the Self, i.e. Self-stabilization. However, the pain over the loss still remains; the alignment to the cyberworld is only a patch on a wound that is still bleeding. The same holds true for the loss of the real partner, which is only covered by this alignment to his or her virtual Self, a wound that is still eliciting psychic pain. To overcome the psychic pain due to the loss of the real partner, the Self needs to align again to the real world, shifting back from its abnormal alignment to the virtual world.

CX Clinical case: The Self and the community

We have already introduced CX. Here is some additional information provided during the first interviews. CX is 24 years old, the eldest of three children; she lives by herself and is trying to obtain a postgraduate degree to be able to work. She does not actually know what she would like to do, whether she wants to remain in the academic world or move into another work environment. She feels depressed, obsessed with the idea of having to know everything about her ex-boyfriend, whom she stopped dating about a year earlier; she controls him minute after minute on Fb. She sometimes happens to meet him because they graduated from the same university and attend the same master's degree course; if this happens, she vomits uncontrollably. She hardly eats anymore, drinks a lot, does not hang out with anyone and spends the rest of the day on her smartphone waiting to 'see' the news on his profile and on all his contacts. She keeps a diary of his contacts and cross-references them to get as much information as possible. Since everyone posts everything, it is not difficult for her to get real-time information about the events he participates in.

She takes various medications prescribed by a psychiatrist, but they do not help improve her mood or soothe her obsessiveness.

Obviously, she used Google to make a self-diagnosis of compulsive use of social networks and monitors the drugs that now she would like to discontinue.

Her whole family engaged in periods of individual/family analysis, because it is 'good' (she thinks) for all of them, to have someone to help you in time of need.

In order to recover from the separation from DY, she tries to date other guys, but after a couple of hours spent together, they all vanish; if she tries to find them, she is systematically told that she is heavy and too much aloof. In fact, she is constantly trying to restore a 'flesh and blood' contact with someone, calling up all the contacts in her address book. But it does not work. CX fantasizes about the relationship until the moment she meets someone, but when this happens, she gets bored, disappointed, and shuns the relationship by taking refuge in DY's Fb page, which she finds much more interesting.

Ego-syntonic Fb control

This story, especially the details of her control through Fb, which can be characterized as reiterated stalking, is ego-syntonic and fills the sessions. Photos, events, phrases, likes and shares are the subject of a careful and meticulous analysis and interpretation on her part.

What is not in tune during the sessions is her mood, which is extremely variable and not consistent with the story. She can quickly shift from a maniac stance to depression during the same session. These swings seem to be related to the degree of anxiety she has to manage when she is away from Fb, which only subsides when she is on her ex-boyfriend's profile. She says:

> It is as if I'm calming my anxiety by watching him on Fb, knowing what he is doing, whom he's with, where he goes. It is as if I don't want to get rid of him. It is as if I'm afraid I will no longer have this thought that fills my life the way he filled it. So, I drink, I smoke, I control him, and that is enough for me. But if I meet him in the real life, like the day before yesterday, when I accidentally met him at a concert with a young woman, I get so distressed that I vomit all the time and the only idea I have to calm my jealousy and envy is to spy on this woman too.

By accommodating her narrative about the life of the other through Fb, *as if* it really was the life of the other shown off through the SNs, we start working on her sense of exclusion elicited by not being part of his life and her sense of inclusion (illusory because in fact she only looks at it) derived from living the various moments posted on Fb together with the community. It is impossible for her to give up this control, namely her control of her beloved object. She knows that she will vomit if she sees him in a post with someone, but she knows the only way she has to triumph over him is to control him without being exposed.

Obviously, each post arouses new fantasies that fuel her sense of exclusion and her desire to have more news to feel 'inside' the network of posted information.

What about her dreams? She dreams about what she supposedly believes to belong to his real life, even if she has only seen it on the web. So, she dreams about his group of friends, the news they exchange, his supposed new love affairs and their photos. There is a perfect osmosis between her online life and her inner world. It is hard for the therapist to distinguish these boundaries.

The patient's shows that what happens online is just as real as what happens offline. Both dimensions feed her dreams, fantasies, and expectations. It is difficult to define the real and virtual Self as opposing labels. Privacy vanishes in a sort of mimesis facilitated by the many contacts offered by Fb that she can make her own and through which she intrudes into her ex-boyfriend's reality.

CX does not accept being excluded from his life, she would like to know the reasons, but she does not dare enquire about them for fear of feeling inadequate in his presence. She repeatedly dreams of meeting him and asking him, but in the dream she runs away at the very moment of the answer, *perhaps for fear of being hurt*, she guesses. So, she entrusts Fb with the task of controlling the nature of his relationships.

She has drawn up a ranking of likes and shares that is the liking index he has among his female friendships. And these become the target of her control.

After a few months of therapy centred on these feelings of exclusion and lack of boundaries, she perceives that Fb does not provide her with the bond she would like to have with him; in fact, the casual physical contact with DY, who is dating another woman, triggers her obsessive thoughts of anger and revenge against both of them.

Indistinct I–You–We

In her fantasy, CX is always at the centre of triangular situations that make her lose her centre. She can easily talk about these Oedipal triangles, which were deeply analyzed during the sessions. But this does not at all reduce her compulsion and all her withdrawal symptoms. The analyst thinks that this conflict is not between her intrapsychic instances, but it seems to be interpsychic, i.e. based on areas of non-recognition of the Self–Other relationship with easily permeable mutual boundaries. This is precisely enabled by the virtual nature of Fb: the possibility to dilute relationships to a single matrix of global and indistinct belonging. It is exactly what the patient is looking for: *I–You–We* are indistinct and confused and the transparency of the web, the absence of privacy and the continuous showing off maintain this illusion.

During the first months of therapy, we try together to delimit the boundaries of her Self, but it is an impossible mission: it is *as if* her Self has protrusions everywhere. Wherever she is, the group is too. It is difficult for the psychoanalyst to feel alone in the session room with CX; it is like being with many other people, constantly clarifying the *I–You–We* in the analysis room.

This situation does not result in major splits of the Self, with forgotten and unintegrated parts, and not even in strong identifications with one character or another one. This may suggest the presence of multiple selves or the systematic construction of aliases to camouflage her control.

She is always very lucid and systematic (good integration) in her description of the events followed on Fb as well as in talking about her dreams. An example: during a quiet session, she tells about her dream of a love triangle

(CX, DY, and the other one) which then accommodates a fourth female person who palpates her, touches her, who is very sympathetic with her. They like each other with conflicting feelings of desire and fear of intimacy.

This provides transferential indications pointing to some indistinct traumatophilic element and also to the need for physical and mental contact perceived as a threat to her psycho-physical integrity. The psychoanalyst does not voice this intuition related to the anguish present in her dreams; in fact, this possible traumatophilic element is unknown at the moment and seems to be related to the group: she wants contact with the group, but she fears its judgement.

In the meantime, in her offline life, she browses through her contacts and gets in touch with old acquaintances. These are fleeting appointments that make her disappointed or irritated. Disappointed when she is not chosen, irritated when she learns that they already have other stable ties. By recognizing her emotions aroused by the 'here and now' of the physical encounter, even DY and the world that revolves around him begin to change.

In her dreams, anger, disappointment, insults, swearing and violence appear. Her dreams conjure up a totally different world from the one spied on Fb. She is surprised. It seems a reversal into an opposite direction: through her dreams, the world of Fb is tinged with violence and aggressiveness. In fact, she begins to distinguish her life on Fb from that of her dreams characterized by primordial instinctual elements in which she recognizes herself: anger, violence, eroticism, sadism. Until one day, after about six months of analysis, a detail of her dream attracts the therapist's attention. In this dream, CX is with DY to talk and finally clarify the situation; he proposes they should go to Z's home, so they take the car and move. While driving, the car spins out of control; they cannot brake, it may crash into Z's fence or bump into other cars parked there. But while all this is happening, DY is gone.

She says that she does not really want to talk to DY because he always disappears; she also leaves some comments about the manic nature of her dream (the car going crazy). *The place where they were heading* attracts the analyst's attention, who asks if the place in her dream really exists and if she recognizes it. Her answer brings up the story of her childhood. She answers:

> *This place is where I and my family and many other families spent the summer holidays and all our free time, all together, guided by a spiritual leader who helped us to grow up well.*

Community dimension

They lived all together in a sharing and community dimension. Everything belonged to everyone. The same guiding principles were applied to all community members who had to adapt to them. Every decision was a group decision; there was no individual will because this was included in the will of the leader. The children grew up happy, they were always together, they played a lot, they were all friends, and there were no contrasts. Moreover, every morning there were collective psychotherapy sessions; others were provided during the day for individuals, couples, families, and groups. Everyone had their own therapy space with the leader. The community members were not allowed to omit or hide any details of their lives, and sex was only allowed for married couples.

After listening to this story, many of the things the patient shared during the analysis start to become clearer. Above all, the *ego-syntonic element* of the symptom is clear: in this community, '*showing up*' was a duty, alongside *transparency* and a *lack of privacy* and *intimacy*. When sex was not formally accepted, it was lived in secret and with guilt. CX says that, as teenagers, they flirted at night, but it was a nightmare because in the morning the whole community knew about it, and they had to respond to the leader who publicly disapproved of their behaviour.

After this story, the sessions completely change. First, she gets depressed and cries all the time. Her parental figures appear in her dreams. The ties become brutal, sadistic, animalistic. Fb is no longer attractive. Her thoughts revolve around her former community life and she revisits and strips it of all the idealization she has used to disguise it.

Her dreams are filled with little animals that no one cares about; they are always on the verge of dying, and she struggles to take care of them. They are small parts of her Self stripped of the authenticity of perceptions and full of interpretations.

> *You were never sure of anything, she says; not even Mom or Dad could tell me if a certain thing was right or wrong; you had to ask the leader. They used the same kind of parenting manual for all parents, filled with good intentions. As long as I was a kid, everything was fine. I had no wishes; I didn't express a thought; the common thought was my thought. The problems started when I became a teenager. My body was changing, faced with the need for contact, the choice of the future and of my friends. I was constantly scolded and shamed by the community because I was rebellious. And so, I dreamed of running away or of the leader dying and getting rid of him.*

Actually, when this happened (the death of the leader), the community members continued to hang out and meet on a regular basis because they didn't have a defined identity outside their community life; they couldn't adapt to life outside the community (the offline life, where the online life was the community, she says) and independently choose their own future.

The boundaries of the Self, the private space, the form and content of her Self, have been totally reshaped by this experience, which was/is her life experience. This is her Self: extended, crowded, full of holes and mending in order to keep it together and avoid fragmentation. The sudden separation from her fiancé, with the abrupt feeling of being excluded from the life of the other, would have led to a major tearing of her Self if Fb had not provided the container that gave her continuity, the sense of belonging to a community.

The complexity of the Self: Object–subject Self

The complexity of the Self comes through these continuous inclusion and exclusion dynamics, camouflages, and distinctions; it builds its boundaries through the *I–You–We game.*
A dream from this period:

> *I am in the bathroom and I am looking at myself in the mirror. A lady opens the door, comes in and sits on the toilet; I protest, telling her that I was there first, but she doesn't care and relieves herself. I leave the door open out of spite so that everyone can see her, but then I am scolded by the head of human resources.*

She associates our evacuation sessions with people from her past who took away all the privacy she needed. She recognizes that she has adopted a community-related habit: the door is always open, and everything is in sight. It is like on Fb, where everything is always in view and the door is always open. Her Self was too open and everyone could invade it.

The sessions provide her with a private and non-shared container (without the group) in which she can experience a new style of functioning through a dual rhythm. And she repeatedly and obsessively dreams of travelling, always with suitcases full of stuff; she gets anguished because the stuff she has to carry is too much, and does not fit in her suitcases (we will elaborate on this dream in Chapter 6).

This is the metaphor of the Self too full of things that do not belong to her. An object Self that does not belong to her while she is desperately searching for a subject Self that provides her with a stable identity (capable of emotional ties but also of professional choices). The Self subject encountered now in the analysis is sometimes a frightening ugly toad or features mummified lizards forgotten by all, little ugly graveyard birds, *as if* the primitive part of her Self (or minimal part) has not evolved, hidden, isolated, mummified until adolescence.

The explosion of her sexual desire with adolescence provided the Self with a new transformative vigour that pushed her at loggerheads with the community. The primitive Self that she tapped into towards the final phase of the analysis appears in a distressing dream in which two eggs are laid by two monstrous birds. One is discarded, thrown away because it is empty, rotten, ugly; the other is washed and helped to develop. The monstrosity of these origins has not prevented her from growing up and adapting to life through the defences she has managed to build. The community life, with its rich ties and events, provided her with contents and experience, which she was able to revisit through the analysis, keeping what she felt belonged to her and letting go of the 'ballast' that weighed her down.

Towards the end of the analysis, she dreams of being in a music therapy session, but she does not understand the music; she can follow its rhythm, but she does not know the music; in her dream, she is given some images that help her find her direction and rhythm. She says that the group sessions in which she participated were preceded by music, and then the leader interpreted the sensations felt. Instead, our analysis has allowed her to abandon these contents, to find again the pleasure of her cognitive and sensorial functions and to recognize the emotions connected to her different experiences.

Once her endoperceptive function is restored (first underestimated with respect to her exoperceptive function) and the rhythm and privacy of her Self is recovered, we can work on the image of her Self and on its identity (professional) so that she can find her place in the labour world.

Considerations about the treatment

What does this case story tell us about the Self in general? The Self seeks relations. No matter what, where, and how. Relations stabilize the Self. They extend beyond the physical and mental Self to the world beyond the Self and its body.

One can thus speak of world–Self relation. The Self aligns and adapts itself to the world, to its environmental, social, and cultural context. Our patient aligned herself strongly to her partner, which stabilized her otherwise vulnerable Self. Relation through alignment, it is nothing special. We relate to the music by aligning ourselves to the rhythm and beat of the music, relation through alignment. And alignment is intrinsically bound to time and space; it is referred to as temporospatial alignment. As we synchronize our movements with the rhythm and beat of the music, we synchronize our own mental life with the mental and physical life of others as our patient to her fiancée. Here, this world–Self alignment is a fiancé–Self alignment; this relation is intrinsically temporospatial as time and space are the 'common currency' of the world, others, Self, and brain.

These are some take-home lessons. The Self is neither mental nor bodily. It is neither encapsulated in some mysterious mind, nor based on our body. The Self extends beyond mind and body. It extends to the world; it synchronizes with the world; through this temporospatial alignment, the Self is intrinsically relational and stabilizes itself. In turn, this alignment shapes the Self's relation to the body, i.e. its embodiment; in fact, our patient stopped eating once she was no longer aligned and related to her fiancée.

Therefore, the relation to the world, the world–Self relation, shapes the body–Self relation and not the other way around; the world–Self relation features a much broader temporospatial range and extension than the body–Self relation that is nested and contained within the former one just as a smaller Russian doll is nested within the next larger one; they have a similar shape, but a different size.

If this broader temporospatial extension of the world–Self relation is disrupted, as in the case of separation, the Self is restricted to the next smaller Russian doll, the body–Self relation; this is the moment when bodily symptoms appear. Due to this shift into a smaller Russian doll, the temporospatial frame and coordinates of the subject's mental life become restricted, which is experienced as a restricted subjective space of the Self which ultimately results in anxiety. Imagine you are standing in an extremely tight space where you barely fit in; over time, you will certainly develop anxiety over the feeling that you may never get out from there and that your Self is threatened. Time is also shorter; the time span of past and future is more restricted to the present without the ability to mentally and virtually extend it into the future; you may become anxious and/or lose confidence about a future for your Self resulting in depression.

How is it possible to escape from this rather narrow temporospatial frame of the body–Self relationship? It is possible to build and construct a virtual and more extended temporospatial frame by reverting to the internet and searching for your partner there so as to maintain your alignment with him/her, albeit in a virtual way. However, in this case, the virtual world–Self relationship is somewhat fragile, like a larger Russian doll that is fragile and cracks so that the smaller Russian doll can no longer be properly contained and nested in a stable way.

This carries major implications for psychotherapy. We suggest that the psychotherapy was successful in this case because the temporospatial frame of the subject was re-shifted and reverted from the cyberworld back to the real world. The Self of the patient was enabled to envisage possible alignments to the real world beyond the one of her lost partner. The psychotherapy was an alignment therapy; it shifted the alignment from the body or the cyberworld back to the real world. Therefore, the psychotherapist needs to work with time and space, extending the limited temporospatial dynamics of the patients beyond their body and the cyberworld to the real world. We assume that the real success factor in psychotherapy of the Self is the manipulation of the subject's temporospatial frame on both the neural and mental levels. If we better understand the neural mechanisms of the world–Self alignment, including its temporospatial features, we can target the world–Self alignment in more specific ways, including biological and psychotherapeutic treatments. This means that the psychotherapy of the Self will ultimately converge into what we describe as 'temporospatial psychotherapy'.

Notes

1 Generation X (1965–1979), Net generation (1980–1989), i Generation (1990–1999), Generation C (2000+). See: Rosen L. (2011). Poke Me: How Social Networks Can

Both Help and Harm Our Kids. *American Psychological Association 119th Annual Convention Washington D.C.*, August 4–7, 2011. In www.fenichel.com/pokeme.shtml For more: https://www.pewresearch.org/internet/2010/12/16/generations-2010/

2 The Oxford English Dictionary defines reality foremost as 'the quality of being real or having an actual existence' and supplements this with a definition of real as 'having objective existence', and finally to exist as having 'place in the domain of reality'. *Oxford English Dictionary.* 2nd Edition online, 1989.

3 A digital-technology expert or enthusiast (a term of pride as self-reference, but often used disparagingly by others). See more: https://www.dictionary.com/browse/geek

4 A person who is extremely interested in one subject, especially computers, and knows a lot of facts about it. See more: https://dictionary.cambridge.org/it/diziona rio/inglese/nerd

5 Some studies have highlighted a number of potential negative correlates of extensive SNS usage. For instance, the results of an online survey of 184 Internet users indicated that people who use SNS more in terms of time spent on usage were perceived to be less involved with their real life communities [71]. This is similar to the finding that people who do not feel secure about their real-life connections to peers and thus have a negative social identity tend to use SNSs more in order to compensate for this [37]. Moreover, it seems that the nature of the feedback from peers that is received on a person's SNS profile determines the effects of SNS usage on wellbeing and self-esteem. (Kuss & Griffiths, 2011, p. 3537)

References

Blau, I. (2011). Application use, online relationship types, self-disclosure, and internet abuse among children and youth: implications for education and internet safety programs. *Journal Educational Computing Research*, 45(1):95–116.

Chakraborty, A. (2016). Facebook Addiction: An Emerging Problem. *American Journal of Psychiatry Residents' Journal*, 11(12):7–9.

Gabbard, G. (2001). Cyberpassion: E-rotic transference on the internet. *Psychoanalytic Quarterly*, 70:719–737.

Gencer, S. L., & Koc, M. (2012). Internet Abuse among Teenagers and Its Relations to Internet Usage Patterns and Demographics. *Educational Technology & Society*, 15(2): 25–36.

Gibbs, P.L. (2007). Reality in Cyberspace: Analysands' Use of the Internet and Ordinary Everyday Psychosis. *Psychoanalytic Review*, 94:11–38.

Griffiths, M. D. (1995). *Adolescent gambling*. London: Routledge.

Griffiths, M. D. (2000). Internet addiction—time to be taken seriously? *Addiction Research*, 8:413–418.

Hardey, M., & Atkinson, R. (2018). Disconnected: non-users of Information Communication Technologies. *Sociological research online*, 23(3):553–571.

Hartman, S. (2012). Cybermourning: Grief in flux from object loss to collective immortality. *Psychoanalytic Inquiry*, 32:454–467.

Kaes, R. (2008). Définitions et approches du concept de lien. *Adolescence*, 3(65):763–780.

Kuss, D.J., & Griffiths, M. D. (2011). Online Social Networking and Addiction—A Review of the Psychological Literature. *International Journal Environment Research Public Health*, 8:3528–3552.

Lemma, A. (2010). An Order of Pure Decision: Growing up in a Virtual World and the Adolescent's Experience of Being-in-A-Body. *Journal American Psychoanalytic Association*, 58:691–714.

Lemma, A. (2015). Psychoanalysis in times of technoculture: Some reflections on the fate of the body in virtual space. *The International Journal of Psychoanalysis*, 96:569–582.

Leménager, T., Gwodz, A., Richter, A., Reinhard, I., Kämmerer, N., Sell, M., & Mann, K. (2013). Self-Concept Deficits in Massively Multiplayer Online Role-Playing Games Addiction. *European Addiction Research*, 19:227–234.

Lévy, P. (1997). *Collective Intelligence: Mankind's Emerging World in Cyberspace*. Cambridge, MA: Perseus.

Morahan-Martin, J. (2008). Internet abuse: Emerging trends and lingering questions. In A. Barak (Ed), *Psychological aspects of cyberspace: Theory, research, applications* (pp. 32–69). Cambridge, UK: Cambridge University Press.

Meerkerk, F.J., Van Den Eijnden, R. J., & Farretsen, H. F. (2006). Predicting compulsive Internet use: It's all about sex. *CyberPsychology & Behavior*, 9:95–103.

Pirandello, L. (2016). *Uno, nessuno, centomila*. Milano: Oscar Mondadori.

Rosen, C. (2007). Virtual friendship and the new narcissism. Summer 2007. *The New Atlantis*. www.TheNewAtlantis.com.

Rosen, L.D. (2011). Poke Me: How Social Networks Can Both Help and Harm Our Kids. *American Psychological Association 119th Annual Convention Washington D. C.*, August 4–7 2011. www.fenichel.com/pokeme.shtml.

Ryan, T., Chester, A., Reece, J., & Xenos, S. (2014). The uses and abuses of Facebook: A review of Facebook addiction. *Journal of Behavioral Addictions*, 3(3):133–148.

Sand, S. (2007). Future Considerations. *Psychoanalytic Review*, 94:83–97.

Schirmacher, W. (2007). Net Culture. *Psychoanalytic Review*, 94:141–149.

Spagnolo, R. (2017). An Unexpected Pathway for Interpsychic Exchange: Music in the Analysis of Young Adult. In B.N. Seitler, & K.S. Kleinman (Eds), *Essays from Cradle to Couch* (pp.341–357). New York: Astoria, IP Books.net.

Suler, J. (2008). Cybertherapeutic theory and techniques. In: A. Barak (Ed.), *Psychological Aspects of Cyberspace: Theory, Research, Applications* (pp. 102–128). Cambridge: Cambridge University Press.

Turkle, S. (1984). *The second self: Computers and the human spirit*. New York: Simon & Schuster.

Turkle, S. (1995). *Life on the screen: Identity in the age of the internet*. New York: Simon & Schuster.

Turkle, S. (1997). *Life on the screen: Identity in the age of the internet*. New York: Touchstone.

Turkle, S. (2002). *Whither psychoanalysis in a computer culture?* Paper originally presented as the 2002 Freud Lecture at The Sigmund Freud Society, Vienna, May 6. Published on KurzweilAI.net, October 23 2002.

Walther, B. (1996). Computer-mediated communication. Impersonal, interpersonal, and hyperpersonal. *Interaction Communication Research*, 23:1–43.

Young, K. S. (1996). Addictive use of the internet: a case that breaks the stereotype. *Psychological Report*, 79: 899–902.

Young, K. S. (1999). Internet addiction: Evaluation and treatment. *British Medical Journal*, 7:351–352.

Chapter 4

The Self between art and madness

We now resume what we elaborated on in the previous chapter, i.e. the Self and the world.

The Self is about alignment, alignment to the environment. We showed that the Self is about time and space, that we align ourselves to our environmental context in terms of space and time. An artist who showed this beautifully in his paintings is Salvador Dalí. He depicts various, sometimes bizarre, time and space constellations in his paintings (which partly come from his dreams). The purpose of this chapter is to sketch the artistic nature of the Self as one of its core features; this is also central for psychoanalysis as well as therapeutically, as we will show. Art can be used as therapy for temporospatially disordered minds and non- or dys-aligned brains; art is life, life is the Self, the disorder introduced by subjectivity may be repaired and corrected only by the Self.

The tightly-knit weave of the narrating Self

In January 1947, after nine years of internment, Artaud returned to the stage of the Parisian theatres to represent, with a long monologue, all the loneliness of the artist and of the man who emerged from hell. The following month, on February 2, 1947, he began to write 'The Man Suicided by Society' at the Orangerie, in front of four self-portraits by Van Gogh.

'No one has even written, painted, sculpted, modeled, built, or invented, excepted literally to get out of the hell' (Artaud, 1947/1976, p. 60), he wrote thinking of Van Gogh's life. The book is a brief journey into the madness of the artist seen through Artaud's suffering. The brief journey of a suffering Self through the pain of the other to make the artistic momentum survive.

In 1947, the full text of O. Wilde's *De profundis* was published in England, edited by the writer's son. It is a work taken from the letter sent from jail to Bosie (Lord Alfred Douglas) and entrusted to his friend Ross. *De profundis* is the only literary product written by O. Wilde in the two years he spent in Reading prison (from 1895 to 1897). The man survived imprisonment, not the artist. Something was definitively destroyed in jail; his torn Self would no longer be capable of any expression.

DOI: 10.4324/9781003221876-5

In 1947, at the age of 16, Alda Merini was admitted to an asylum for the first time for a month. Confusion, madness, suffering, they began to march together without ever leaving her. Unceasingly and relentlessly with a river of words and through the gift of poetry, she tried to stitch the '*shreds of her Self*' continuously fragmented by the experience of delusion.

These are random and insignificant time coincidences, but through the stories of these three artists, they may bring about some reflections on aspects of the Self linked both to its narrative and to its suffering. Is the former ancillary to the latter? The human story of many artists is intertwined with the thread of poetics into a '*tightly-knit*' weave that leaves no room for suffering or delusions. This *tightly-knit* weave is the metaphor of the narrating Self that intertwines the threads of reality, memory and suffering, braiding, unthreading and recreating to adapt to the world.

Bacon (Sylvester, 2012) suggested how difficult it was to eliminate the narration between one character and the other, because as soon as several characters are put on the same canvas, a story unfolds, which speaks louder than the painting and claims to be told. Bacon, unbeknownst to himself, seems to be in line with the evidence from neuroscience, i.e. that all abstract works activate more limited parts of the visual brain than narrative and figurative art (Zeki, 1999). Hence figuration is already a narrative.

The creative process that engages the artist's brain in shaping physical and psychic reality is the same as any other creative process of any human brain (Kandell, 2012). If the creative process is intrinsic to the functioning of the brain, it is therefore the same for all human beings; the difference with the artist, with the talent of the genius, consists in the construction of subjectivity, that is, the difference itself 'is' subjectivity:

> Subjectivity is a relentlessly constructed narrative. The narrative arises from the circumstances of organisms with certain brain specifications as they interact with the world around, the world of their past memories, and the world of their interior.
>
> (Damasio, 2018, p. 159)

The Self builds continuity, composing and narrating. It is the narrating subject and object of the narrative. In the dream, the Self is simultaneously the subject and the object, the same as in art and psychotic delusion.

When the narrating subject loses continuity, it shatters into psychotic thought; instead, when the object of the narration takes over, a huge wave of new realities swells up. Psychosis and creation often walk hand in hand, an artistic combination where we can glimpse the complexity of the structure of the Self that does not easily get caught in the meshes of our neuroscientific descriptions.

The endless work of the Self

As to this complexity, we do not know from a psychoanalytical nor from a neuroscientific point of view where to place the artist's suffering in the production of an artwork, while we manage to place the delusion or dissociation induced suffering in a psychopathological framework.

Instead, readers recognize this affliction in the silent works that speak to them, eliciting dormant, pre-reflective aesthetic consonances.

We are not describing the evocative value of an image, a word, a melody. Nor are we questioning the universal characteristics of art (Ramachandran & Hirstein, 1999), that is, the invariant traits of creativity that turn an artistic product into a work of art.

Through the genius of the artist, we are describing the complex dynamics of the Self, its transparent essence in actively building its space–time continuity, so as not to hinder the flow and visibility of its contents that sometimes come to us as an artistic product.

According to Bacon, the artist invents traps to capture living data (Sylvester, 2012). We would like to add that the artist may be continually faced with 'a surplus' that goes beyond the binding, constructing and recomposing dynamics of the Self. And this overload deforms, shatters the Self, and breaks its continuity, i.e. the original attachment of the subject to its being (Gambazzi, 1999).

The endless work of the Self to sew up the shreds of subjectivity torn by suffering may be silent, as while sleeping/dreaming, when the various brain regions communicate to consolidate or erase memories (Houldin, 2019; Langille, 2019), or it may come up in words, images, music, or in an artistic product. By capturing our attention, art shows how the complexity of the Self, expressed through the work of art, transcends its structure; that is, it goes beyond the configuration that the Self has taken up in that given person. Finally, we may say that the Self, '*shaped by artistic talent*', transcends the very existence of the artist through the artistic product. But if we place the Self back to its origins, that is, at the level of the subject and not of art transcendence, we can find its roots, saturated in the world of affects:

> There is a parallel mental world that accompanies all those images, often so subtle that it does not demand any attention for itself, but occasionally so significant that it alters the course of the dominant part of the mind, sometimes arrestingly so. That is the parallel world of affect, a world in which we find feelings traveling alongside the usually more salient images of our mind.
>
> (Damasio, 2018, p. 99)

As psychoanalysts, we easily recognize these redundancies, as, for example, in psychotic delusions, neurotic conflicts, obsessive silent rituals, which reveal the broken thread that unravels the texture. We are trained to see the 'Self at work'[1] and therefore we should be able to see the ingenious creations inspired by madness, through the dynamics of the Self and its redundancies. Or rather the suffering of the genius inhabited by art that appears to us as madness.

Do we consider artistic genius as a gift, a natural talent, because we define it through artistic work? But how would 'the artistic genius' appear if seen from inside the subject?

In *History of madness*, Foucault (2009) provides some examples. What do artistic genius and suffering have in common? Two things: generating and destroying symbionts.

The artistic genius and suffering are strongly attached to each other; they can only mutually express themselves in the biography (life experience) they have built, that is the life of the artist, part of which is the artistic product.

Oscar Wilde writes in *De profundis*:

> We are no longer in art concerned with the type. It is with the exception that we have to do. I cannot put my sufferings into any form they took, I need hardly say.
>
> Art only begins where Imitation ends, but something must come into my work, of fuller memory of words perhaps, of richer cadences, of more curious effects, of simpler architectural order, of some aesthetic quality at any rate.
>
> (Wilde, 1947/2001, p. 25)

It is this element—*but something must come into my work ... some aesthetic quality*—that has long since questioned the birth of the work of art. For Zeki (1993), art extends the cognitive functions of the brain. For Kandell (2012), art improves our understanding of emotional and social signals, which are important for our survival.

Can the artists' madness be considered a limit or a resource for their artistic genius?

Certainly, madness does not account for the birth of a work; it can only shape it or fill it with content. Madness gathers the pathological deformations of the Self and tells about the mimesis with the object of madness (Dalí, 1942) through the artwork. In the work of art, we see the Self and its objects at the same time; this contemporaneity (ambiguity—Sylvester, 2012) allows us to grasp something of us, and of the other, in the artistic product, which facilitates its fruition.

From the origin towards the complexity of the Self

As psychoanalysts, we are also trained to question the past and retrace it through transference; in the session, the past takes on the 'just happened' form, while in the patient, it takes on the timeless recursive form of the child. Through the slow psychoanalytic work of reconnecting near and far experiences, we are sometimes able to restore continuity to the Self and iden-tify the path between the historical imprinting of the trace and its actualiza-tion in the symptom. In spite of this, there is still the open question of what part of the past remains active in the present; in artists, through the constant exercise of these traces, this part produces signs that shine like tracers scat-tered in the artworks and that resonate in us guiding us through their interpretation.

Perhaps, the answer is their ability to go beyond the perception of the visible (Merleau Ponty, 1968), or their ability to directly contact what is perceived and convey the hallucinatory creation through delusions. But perhaps and more likely, through the work of art, one day we will no longer be able to know what madness was, that is, we will no longer be able to read (and find) the subject and his or her story through its traces (Foucault, 2009).

Traces, metaphorical configurations, and images recomposed in a poem or a painting propel biography to infinity and no longer belong to it, while madness has a different and sad fate. Merini writes in her diary:

> In mental illness, the primitive part of our being, the creeping, prehistoric part, comes to the surface and so we find ourselves to be reptiles, mam-mals, fish but no longer human beings.
>
> (Merini, 1997, p. 68)

The artist, inhabited by madness, tries to find the human through words, images, or music, to retrieve some traumatic element (oozing suffering), so that it can be assimilated into a more evolved representational and symbolic structure. But if the structure of the Self is frayed by the too many dis-continuities experienced in life, this retrieval effort is bound to fail.

As well described by Merini, who spent much of her life in a mental asylum, like Artaud:

> You always end up in some kind of rule because man is a finite person who cannot see infinity, who has no infinity in front of him; from the moment he is born, he knows he has to die, even if he doesn't take it into account [...] You have to stay in the pedestrian crossings of life and con-tinue to be a child even when you are an adult.
>
> (De Lillo, 2013)

Looking for rules, looking for continuity, looking for a stable structure is part of normal development, which is not always able to contain the surplus of talent and of madness.

Being delirious (delirium) etymologically recalls the Latin word '*lira*', furrow, preceded by '*de*' which means overflowing, *going beyond*, trespassing; according to the words of the poet, it means not staying on the pedestrian crossing of life; it is trespassing in the power of infinity with the knowledge to find the finite. Or rather, knowing to find again the finite nature of the human being enclosed in a suffering body or, simply, this finite nature 'locked' in the slow and inexorable flow of time that directs birth towards death. This is Self-embodiment: the finite structure of the body, which limits the infinite possibilities of access to talent. As for Beethoven, whose daily struggle with his progressive deafness put him in contact with the limits that the body imposed on his genius:

> Such incidents (*dealing with deafness, we add*) drove me almost to despair; a little more of that and I would have ended my life—it was only my art that held me back. So, I endured this wretched existence, truly wretched for so susceptible a body, which can be thrown by a sudden change from the best condition to the very worst.
>
> (Van Beethoven, 1802)

If the Self was an illusion, it would have infinity at its disposal. But being incarnated in a body, destined to die, it binds it to finiteness, to death.

The 'zero' time of poetry (Merini described this in many poems, Merini, 1951/1997) is something immobile that awaits its becoming. If 'something' happens there, in that point, in that moment, life manifests itself.

It does not matter if 'that point' is the damnation of hell (and the list of artists would be long); where it surfaces, there is life marked by the passing of time; that point and that moment mark the escape from the irrepresentable void, which is synonymous with death, as for Oscar Wilde after his prison experience. There, where it comes to the surface, *we find the origins and the becoming of the Self.*

The origins and the becoming of the Self

Many works of art feature this indissoluble combination between the slow pace of death that erodes the boundaries of life and the feeble and painful manifestations of life that tries to gain ground on death. It is a relentless struggle where madness and art can coexist.

> Every child has his or her own stable ground of life, but where a poet is born no one knows.
>
> (Merini, 1995/2011, p. 21)

The sailing ships indeed; an emerging Self, always laboriously brought back to the surface, which leaps and bounces above the silent waters of the temptation of eternal rest; a Self which is prevented from sinking through a word, a brushstroke, a note.

An attempt, always with an uncertain outcome, on the edge of the definitive loss of the Self.

It will suffice to think of the black crows looming over the wheat fields: beyond that image, we can see the window through which Van Gogh opened his view to the wheat fields, while, under the weight of that leaden sky that corroded him from the inside, he was being pushed into that final shipwreck from which no brushstroke would bring him back to the surface.

After his imprisonment, Oscar Wilde would no longer find words to hook himself to a reality that rebuffed him and whose painful outcome he had predicted:

> Many men on their release carry their prison about with them into the air, and hide it as a secret disgrace in their hearts, and at length, like poor poisoned things, creep into some hole and die.
>
> (Wilde, 1947/2001, p. 8)

Or, again, Artaud, who died and was resuscitated as many times as his electroshocks:

> The electroshock throws me into despair; it takes away my memory, it numbs my thoughts and my heart, it makes me an absent-minded person who feels absent-minded and who goes in search of his own being for weeks, like a dead person next to a living person who is no longer himself, who calls for him to come and into whom he can no longer enter.
>
> (Artaud, 1974/1976, p. 13)

Alda Merini instead survives and seeks life wherever it may manifest itself. She survives and returns to life continuously as an anti-heroic structure[2] that accepts the falls of life and finds a compromise to continue living, unlike the Greek hero who comes on time to meet his destiny and hence his death; in fact, for the anti-hero, this appointment is always postponed, again and again renewing the pain and causing new cancellations or new splits. She wrote:

> I have always felt close to death. I have considered her as a sister since I was a child, because I felt she was a companion of love. I talked to her, I delayed her, I even loved her.
>
> (Merini, 1995/2011, p. 59)

The work of erasing or splitting, even when it is full of delusions, leaves a gap that reveals the affect that can never be completely reduced to representation.

So, the pain is now inside the artistic composition as it once was inside the body. Suffering is inside the artistic expression exactly as it can be in a wrinkle on the forehead (The Pity by Michelangelo), a lowered eyebrow (The Beheading of Saint John the Baptist by Caravaggio), or the open mouth screaming without a word (The Scream by Munch). Suffering is to the artwork what pain is to the posture of the body. Both signifiers are continuously searching for their meaning.

In madness and in the work of art, the one (the signifier) cannot be reduced to the other (the meaning), but they recombine in the subjective perception of the receiver. Hence, maybe, it is the subjective perception of the artwork (and of madness for some non-regulatory aspects) that needs to resonate in the receiver to reconcile the affect and the representation which were originally divided by the contact with suffering.

In the silence (and in the long periods of mutism), the poet waited for the word to come up to organize the mortifying chaos that lived in her.

'Let's pretend that there are small scattered pieces of paper, the inspiration is like breath unsettling the cards, and the stylistic gift recomposes them into new forms'—Merini says in the *Crazy woman next door*. We called these fragments *'shreds of the Self'*.

The artists reassemble the fragments of their Self into exclusive works showing us the complexity of their Self in becoming culture. This is what this young patient tells us in her slow psychotherapeutic work of recovery of her *'shreds of the Self'*.

Shreds of the Self

By Flavia Salierno[3]

Introducing the clinical case

We are going to start with the images. We venture into this like aimless wanderers in unknown lands, full of surprises and wonders. The construction together with the deconstruction of our sensations and feelings find us as mere users of art, which has the task of moving us closer to the unknowable. It is not always necessary to give images a meaning by analyzing their content, but it is possible to merely enjoy the sensations which immediately arise when looking at them.

Here are TX's photos:

From the treatment diary

I met TX at the Drug Addiction Treatment Center where I worked. The first time I saw her, I was amazed by her beauty. Her untidy way of wearing men's and oversized clothes clashed with her graceful appearance. Beautiful, long, and shining hair messily tied up and a clumsy way of walking for a slim and elegant figure. Her first words were enough for me to understand that she was completely unaware of her appearance. Drugs had gained the upper hand over her 'shredded' existence. Despite her young age, TX's existence was already full of lives, moving, changes of schools, pain, lack of references and bases on which subjectivity and continuity can be built.

Fig.4.1

Fig.4.2

Fig.4.3

Fig.4.4

In our first session, TX started telling her story aloud, as if she was reading a book, a novel in which the main character was someone else, distant from her, the result of a vivid imagination, though not hers. I struggled to follow her; the attention I was paying to the load of anguish she was giving me was disturbed by the extremely loud voice she used to tell her story. I felt the distance she put between me and her, an unpassable wall that did not let me ask the questions that I would have liked to ask.

TX is the daughter of an English painter and a 'flower child/hippie'; she moved in with her mother and her partner, when her parents separated. When she was 8, TX resided in a trailer, forced to live with her mother's partner, an ignorant and violent man whom she hated. She started taking drugs when she was 13. At 16 she started to live on her own, working and studying art in high school, while she was living in a van with a man who was much older than her. After the first two years, this man started to hit her, but despite all this, TX enrolled in the Accademia delle belle Arti in Florence, majoring in photography. She ended her relationship with this violent man. Her substance abuse got worse until TX decided to move closer to her father, with a boyfriend, a drug addict like her, who was the only affective handhold she could grab on to. Then she decided to look for help at the Drug Addiction Treatment Center, where she started methadone and was referred to me for psychotherapy.

Construction–deconstruction of drug addiction

TX immediately seemed to agree to meet once a week at the Drug Addiction Treatment Center. I could not see her more often in that setting. I knew that if we had met twice a week, the treatment would have had more continuity and provided a more solid basis to allow for a fuller recovery of her Self. At the same time, I knew that a great help for our work was the possibility for her to regularly get to the centre to take methadone. The Drug Addiction Treatment Center where I worked was in a small town not far from Rome. Since this centre was not in the big city, the staff were able to better follow up with their patients and to have a closer, warmer relationship with them, unlike the same units in Rome. I knew I had a very passionate and motivated team on my side, able to build unique relationships with the patients. Methadone was administered talking to patients, following up on them, putting at ease people that needed the medication.

So, this was an environment/setting that supported the psychotherapeutic work with patients. Winnicott (1971) explains the difference between starting a relationship with an object and the use of the object. In starting a relationship, the subject lets changes occur in her or his Self and lets them be accompanied by a certain degree of physical involvement. TX could 'use' the psychotherapist as well as the centre where she was administered the methadone.

On her arrival, the bare room where we met for our sessions filled up with words which alone were not able to explain the empty or overcrowded world of her life, made up of any kinds of drugs.

Her body, which TX also used as a model for her painting classes, seemed to her distant like her intellectual brightness or the awareness of her clarity of mind, which persisted despite her drug addiction.

TX was very late for our first few appointments, blaming her partner for that because she had to make arrangements with him to go and receive methadone together. I would hear them arriving because of her loud voice when she was greeting everyone and which I felt very disturbing. I knew that the origin of that feeling laid behind the mask TX used to hide her despair. And the shame for being there, for being a 'drug addict'. Indeed, one of the themes she managed to bring into the sessions was the fact that she had never wanted her life to end up like that. TX would have liked to restart, express her art, even though she was no longer able to feel inspired.

The hopelessness that I experienced made me feel the uselessness of my intervention. As unfortunately happens when working as a psychoanalyst, it seemed to me that I would never be able to do anything against such primitive and deeply rooted wounds. And I felt even more hopeless when TX started to miss our appointments, saying that she was not able to wake up, get out of bed, and come there. Nonetheless, I would call her, taking responsibility for this decision, so that she could feel that I was waiting for her and I was thinking about her.

When she managed to come to our sessions, I tried as much as possible to let her recognize the affects, to have a deeper contact with them.

I remember the moments in which TX was able to recover her Self and lowered her voice, getting emotional. Soon after she put distance again between us and from what she was telling me. She spoke very few sentences with a more intimate tone, more connected to her real emotions.

'*I use drugs to detach/break away from my body, from my head, and I can't get do without them*', she said in a low and emotional tone. '*I do many things, I feel fine, I can surely get rid of drugs when I want*', she said out loud and with a distant tone. This alternation made me feel on a rollercoaster; I felt the same struggle she was making in trying to stand like a surfer in a stormy sea. In turn, she felt that I was sharing her struggle in climbing up and down the mountains, and this slowly moved us closer; the relationship with me moved her closer to a better perception of her Self.

TX started to no longer recognize herself in the continuous search for drugs, in the lazy and resigned attitude of the partner she lived with. She urged him to look for a job, desperately asking him to help her and himself to stay away from drugs; to help her get out of bed in the morning, where she would have also remained as a hideaway from her psychic reality, which she experienced as frightening. She knew that this relationship was destined to end. TX was starting to realize that he represented the destroyed and self-destructive part of the Self. TX was starting to understand how much she felt attached to him because maybe for the first time she felt loved. She said:

> He is a good person, maybe too fragile, but good. I can't stand seeing him lying on the couch when the house is falling apart. I can't stand the fact that he's not looking for a job, even if we have to do grocery shopping and we have many things to pay.

I felt TX's first steps towards a closer contact with her Self, no longer far from reality. However, the use of drugs continued, mixed with methadone, and so did my constant concern for her. I was not able to get out of that impasse either, but I remember an image I grabbed to get out of that static condition I felt. TX told me that, with the little money they had, she had bought some wall paints of many different colours. They had spent the whole weekend painting. The girl highlighted the beauty of the colour of the walls in the study she wanted to devote to her artistic works. She was telling me about this with a very loud voice, which suggested that she was not able to contact what she was saying. However, I held on to this wish to paint walls, as if it had been a life vest.

However, TX likes painting, drawing clothes, as well as sewing them and taking pictures; on this common ground, we found the possibility of exploring and moving otherwise unknowable common spaces closer.

Her photos, which she brought me inside a metal box full of her stuff, had an effect that Freud (1919) might have defined as disturbing, but at the same time they gave me an insight that allowed both of us to find a common language that had little to do with words. I was too busy feeling overwhelmed by the frustration of her often-missed appointments or by the concern about the drugs she used, but TX was actually showing me her existence, lost in her life on the edge or spent frequently moving. And then came her photos between us, her poetry, her frozen affectivity, her demand for a look, for being looked at. TX had used a model who looked a lot like her, using her as a mirror.

The relationship with me and the centre where she felt welcomed and taken care of probably gave her a container, the frame within which to keep the shreds of her Self together, otherwise lost in their fragmentation, and the possibility to tell about them and herself, even without any words.

Images and self-portrait

When TX brought me her photos, I was delving into the style and poetics of an American photographer, Cindy Sherman, who really intrigued and motivated me. Not being an art expert allows me to get curious and be engaged freely, with no pre-established dictates.

Through her famous self-portraits, Cindy Sherman (2003) champions her ideas through photography, not the opposite: she uses it to portray the world through her own representation and self-representation.

By wearing the masks also worn by society, Sherman creates a chance to adequately represent herself and others through herself.

She therefore makes a public place of herself, with her photos becoming a public place too where different levels of the Self are exhibited.

Moreover, Sherman uses her own body to mirror what surrounds her. TX uses her body as well, her own image through artistic expression for a transition, namely her self-representation, which is not possible on a conscious level.

She performs this transition on a double track and through a 'double'. The model in her pictures is a woman very similar to her. In some forms of art based on images, these are not at the service of words, but rather words are at the service of images, where words turn into images and images turn into words that can be heard (Chianese & Fontana, 2010).

Navigating freely from the harsh reality of war portrayed in Robert Capa's photos to David LA Chapelle's surreal ones, photography uses images that hook on a fraction of a real moment in order to transform it. Photography represents the merging of the reality and imagination domains, where what is narrated is not what we see but what we want to show by giving an interpretation of it.

TX told me that 'Superfluous', the title she gave to her series of works, was designed to offer a meaning to them and put an emphasis on a certain use of the body as an object. This made me indeed think about how she perceived herself as superfluous and unnecessary. Just like Sherman, TX uses her own body and transformed image as a mediator between her inner and outer world, relying on photography as a transformational object, a thought borrowed from Bollas (1987). Some emotions need an iconic representation to be thought of, and the image is shaped by the forces of the unconscious.

A work of art represents an area between the Self and the external world and the creative process, with its mysteries, has always enthralled psychoanalysts.

In her pictures, Cindy Sherman constructs and deconstructs herself through her own images. It is a reiterated game in which she represents herself in her shapes and levels, but she also seems to be focusing on the other figures, on the representations of others and of herself through those of the others.

TX also uses representations, actually her representations through a 'double', as Frida Kahlo used them as inner healing, through the reconstruction of the Self. In her famous self-portraits, the Mexican painter exhibits the trauma and the strength to rise up again, the pain and the desire to be reborn. Through her art, she overcomes her fragmentation. Frida Kahlo's self-portraits also feature the body in the determined attempt to not get lost in the suffering and the insanity caused by her chronic pain, her bedridden life and her tormented love affair.

Frida Kahlo painted her reality as she felt it and as she lived it. This is the reason why she always refused to define herself as a 'surrealist'. In her 1939 work 'The Two Fridas', both Fridas have their heart exposed in their chest, a symbol of her pain in a dialogue between the Self and a part of her Self (Kahlo, 1939).

TX's dolls probably have the same function: picturing herself through a 'double'. Sherman's and TX's dolls are frozen; they look for recognition in the gaze of others, without which everything seems crystallized. They look for a way to get from mere objects to subjects. The body becomes the carrier of suffering and, in turn, photography becomes the way through which that suffering can be transformed and then portrayed. The body is represented in its stillness, but with the hidden din of the areas of pain.

There is a transition from the first to the third person through self-representation, with the possibility to see inner elements from the outside, which otherwise may not have any boundaries.

Therefore, photography, as a form of art, acts as an intermediary beyond time and space; it uses the body and its transformed image, like a mediator between the inner and outer world.

TX resewed the shreds of the Self through art, through creative production. She sews together pieces of her subjectivity. By looking at her pictures, we retrieve the traumatic element; we feel it vibrate in the vision of its own representation, in its art.

Cindy Sherman paints through photographs, using black and white to make us meditate and feel moved, observe and be astonished, outraged, but also to have fun.

Through photography, TX builds her subjectivity; through her pictures, she pieces together, rearranges and portrays her Self. She tells her story, and, at the same time, she is the object of her story. TX's pain lies behind the stillness of the doll, but the doll helps her rebuild and give continuity to her Self. Representation and rebuilding of the Self, in a process of transformation, in the slow and hard path of subjectivation.

Transitions

In transference and countertransference, the creative and the analytical process proceed simultaneously. In fact, during the analytical process, the analyst acts as a transitional object through the subject's emotional and imaginative fulfilment. This transitional space between the analyst and the patient allows for creativity beyond symbolization.

An intermediate space between the Self and the external world is created through the work of art. TX can set herself free from the overload (drugs) used to hide her emptiness. A space, namely an analytical space, is cleared for the two protagonists to finally meet.

Through transference, the analyst also becomes a means for the artist to add a non-integrated part to the work they do together. Both parts unknowingly contribute to a constant interaction of mind, body, and the environment. The analytical relationship and the one with the Drug Addiction Treatment Center offer TX a primary environment suited to her psychic life and therefore to her creativity. As Meltzer stated, everyone's aesthetic experience is inevitably brought into the psychoanalytic setting, creating a part of the patient's material, which is later processed in the transference between patient and analyst (Meltzer & Williams, 1988).

Some thoughts as a psychoanalyst about the end of the analysis.

I started feeling I could let go of all my thoughts. I felt that all this allowed both of us to breathe, and the patient to better connect with her reality, her own body and her Self. TX ended the relationship with her partner for the sake of both of them, in order to help them quit drugs. She found a job in a garden centre. She had never taken care of plants, but she immediately developed a passion for them and for their beauty.

Beauty, a recurring theme in her conversations and ambitions.

She told me that because of her job at the garden centre and its schedule, she had to stop coming to our sessions. Once more, I felt a sense of frustration, regret, helplessness, fearing this could hurt her again. I felt I was just at the beginning of the work, that I could do so much work with her; then I thought that sometimes it may better to leave some spaces unfilled and that TX was asking me to let her continue alone, to let what had been built settle.

We parted ways, leaving things 'pending', with the idea to start again after a while.

However, I knew that she would still rely on the centre, with which she remained connected over time. I heard from TX to ask permission to publish her pictures and her story.

It was very emotional for us both. TX is no longer using drugs; she sews clothes by her own design, she paints, and she still takes pictures.

Artistic transformation

Emily Dickinson chose to isolate herself from the world, feeling too distant from it. She put her ability to move into the private sphere of her experience. She put her inability to access the world into her poems. She lived a great part of her life locked into a room, which probably functioned as a container within which or thanks to which the poet tried to keep together the 'shreds of the Self'.

TX and all the poets and painters discussed in this chapter belong to different styles, visions, stories, completely different scenarios, but they share their self-representation of pain. The artistic transformation is necessary to go through the shreds of the Self; it provides the opportunity to put them together, to sew them together; it restores a unitary and assembled form to everything that would otherwise be broken down/dismantled and dis-aggregated. Art and beauty feed our brain in the rooms of our private spaces where boundaries are necessary, but in a continuous transformation thanks to their mobility. Everything is an ongoing process, like our path as wanderers, ready to change road if our way tells us so.

What is our Self about? TX's Self reveals it in a paradigmatic way. She externalized or, in other words, outsourced her Self. The drugs took over the role of her substitute Self.

Why? Her real Self was too painful for her to endure. And what do we do when confronted with pain? We try to escape. But what about the escape from our Self? We escape the spatiotemporal bounds of our Self; we beyond or better we get outside of them. This is also visible in Frida Kahlo: she externalizes her own Self beyond her own spatial and temporal boundaries, there where she finds her Self. Nothing can illustrate this better than paintings, whether it be paintings or drugs or something else. The dream world of drugs is so much better to endure; the virtual world of paintings and literature provides a much better substitute for locating the Self with respect to the body and the mind.

So, what is ultimately the Self? The Self is about space and time; it is a virtual space and time that we, in a mental way, develop over time in relation and balance with the environment. If the relation to the environment becomes too harmful due to, for instance, missing, dysfunctional or painful attachment, the Self escapes to save itself. It escapes from itself, that is, from its own inner virtual mental space and time. First, escape is provided by the body: the Self moves from the mind to the body, and the symptoms related to the Self are no longer felt on a mental but on a bodily level resulting in anxiety and somatoform symptoms. The body is the remnant of traumatic experiences; this is well known and has been impressively described by Clara Mucci (2018). However, if the trauma has affected the body, the body no longer provides any escape; it is necessary to virtually go beyond and outside the spatiotemporal confines of the body through drugs, art, and others means; they now provide the escape for the Self to find itself outside its original spatiotemporal boundaries. This is what we see in TX; the therapy illustrates the gradual return of this patient to her own original Self and its spatiotemporal confines from the virtual worlds outside her Self and her body created by drugs and by all the activities related to drugs.

Van Gogh's paintings also show how colours change according to his Self; the more he loses his Self (due to his psychosis), the greater the colour changes in his paintings change. In a way, art is Self-therapy for the artist. For us, as non-artists, it makes us see deeper dimensions of our Self which usually remain hidden and inaccessible.

Great art is like plunging into the depth of the ocean, which is usually concealed on the surface.

So now, what is the Self about? The Self is about spatiotemporal integration; different scales of space and time need to be integrated like waves in the sea. If this integration is disrupted by an external trauma, the Self will search for escape routes from its spatiotemporal features, just like sea waves that find a way around a rock. If the rock is too big, the Self and its spatiotemporal waves are blocked.

Who stands behind all the spatiotemporal boundaries and waves of the Self? We already know this from the previous chapters, it is the brain that is the organization of its waves; that processes and lets the environmental waves flow through. The waves of the Self are brain waves and psychotherapy, whether simple or complex, deals with these waves.

Notes

1 By this we mean that we can recognize the continuous process of construction and transformation of the Self linked to its affective and historical dimension.

2 We have in mind the structure of the anti-hero much celebrated in Literature (from Homer's Thersite to Don Quixote by M. de Cervantes Saavedra, the many characters of Dostovieski and Zeno Cosini by I. Svevo, as well as Papageno in Mozart's Magic Flute, or the modern Frodo of Tolkien's Lord of the Rings). The anti-heroic structure is conceived by Merini as a passive acceptance of the events, in order not to break the link with life and allow for survival. In analytical terms, we may think of these structures as tending 'to the minimum' in terms of mental functioning so as to eliminate the untying force of the death drive (for example the compulsion to repeat, as default functioning, may be considered as one of these minimal elements and it may not work in the direction of the death drive but to maintain a minimum amount of energy to continue living).

3 Psychoanalyst and Psychotherapist in Rome, Italy.
   We would like to thank her for the clinical case and comments.

References

Artaud, A. (1947/1976). *Selected writing. Van Gogh the Man suicided* (p. 483). Berkeley: University of California Press.

Artaud, A. (1974/1976). *Selected writing. Letter to Jacques Latrémolière,* XXXI (p. 437). Berkeley, LA: University of California Press. Translated from: *Oeuvres complètès, Tome XI: lettres écrites de Rodez* (1945–1946) (p. 13). Paris:Gallimard, 1974.

Bollas, C. (1987). *The Shadow of the Object.* New York: Free Association Books, Columbia University Press.

Chianese, D., & Fontana, A. (2010). *Immaginando.* Roma: Franco Angeli.

Dalí, S. (1942). *The secret life of Salvador Dalí.* New York: Dial Press.

Damasio, A. (2018). *The strange order of things.* New York: Pantheon Books.

De Lillo, A. (2013). *The crazy woman next door.* Video movie on Alda Merini's life. Antonietta De Lillo Filmmaker. Rome, Italy.

Freud, S. (1919). *The uncanny. S.E.,* 17: 219–256. London: Hogarth.

Foucault, M. (2009). *History of madness.* London/New York: Routledge.

Gambazzi, P. (1999). *L'occhio e il suo inconscio.* Milano: Raffaello Cortina Editore.

Houldin, E. (2019). Resting state network dynamics across wakefulness and sleep. *Electronic Thesis and Dissertation Repository,* 6397. https://ir.lib.uwo.ca/etd/6397.

Kahlo, F. (1939). *The Two Fridas.* Located in Modern Art Museum, Mexico City, Frida Kahlo Paintings. www.fridakahlo.org.

Kandell, E. R. (2012). *The age of Insight.* New York: Penguin Random House.

Langille, J. J. (2019). Remembering to forget: A Dual role for sleep oscillations in memory consolidation and forgetting. *Frontiers Cellular Neuroscience,* 13(71): 1–21.

Meltzer, D., & Williams, M.H. (1988). *The apprehension of beauty.* London: Karnac.

Merini, A. (1951/1997). La carne ed il sospiro. *Fiore di poesia* (1951/1997). Torino: Einaudi.

Merini, A. (1995/2011). *La pazza della porta accanto.* Milano: Bompiani Editori.

Merini, A. (1997). *L'altra verità.* Milano: Rizzoli.

Merleau Ponty, M. (1968). *The visible and the invisible.* Evanston: Northwestern University Press.

Mucci, C. (2018). *Borderline Bodies.* New York/London: W W Norton & Company.

Ramachandran, V. S., & Hirstein, W. (1999). The science of art a neurological theory of aesthetic experience. *Journal of Consciousness Studies,* 6 (6–7):15–51.

Sherman, C. (2003). *The complete untitled film stills.* New York: MoMA Publications.

Sylvester, D. (2012). *The brutality of the fact. Interview with Francis Bacon.* London: Thames and Hudson.

Van Beethoven, L. (1802). *Heiligenstadt testament.* https://www.all-about-beethoven.com/heiligenstadt_test.html.

Wilde, O. (1947/2001). *De profundis.* eBook Version, Phoenix: Library.org.

Winnicott, D.W. (1971). *Playing and reality.* London/New York: Routledge.

Zeki, S. (1993). *A vision of the brain.* Oxford: Blackwell Scientific Publications.

Zeki, S. (1999). *Inner vision. An exploration of art and the brain.* Oxford/New York: Oxford University Press.

Chapter 5

The Self into the dreams

Conscious experience during sleep

Does the analysis of dreams during psychotherapy bring about new insights?

The following thoughts on the use of dreams during a session relate to dreaming as a vehicle for a broader, and more meaningful, vision of the patient's mind, or the mind in general.

We start from the simple assumption that dreams are always related to the dreamer, as McNamara (2011) writes:

> The single most frequent character in dreams is the Self-the dreamer. The dream, furthermore, is almost always about this Self. The dreamer is virtually always the hero in the dream. The dreamer is virtually always the center of the action. The dreamer is virtually always the character in the dream that experiences some challenge and then undergoes some emotional struggle around the challenge. The dreamer, finally, passes through all these narcissistic, self-centered struggles and melodramas we call dreams only to awaken into the real world each morning.
>
> (McNamara, 2011, p. 1)

So, what are dreams made of, and what do they tell us about our nightlife?

While we are sleeping, the subcortical structures intensely interact with the cortical structures, generating an activity similar to what we experience during the day, even if different in terms of rhythm (cycles of 'delta waves' alternated with cycles of 'sleep spindles', NON-REM–REM sleep) and of the brain structures involved.

Several different functions have been proposed for the NON-REM–REM sleep activity. Langille (2019) analyzes some of them. He proposes to consider memory consolidation; gist extraction, and synaptic homeostasis for NON-REM sleep; as well as cell cleansing and prophylaxis through the metabolic system. While, for REM sleep, he takes into consideration simulation and subsequent habituation to emotional scenes and their memory consolidation; non-declarative memory consolidation and integration of newly encoded

DOI: 10.4324/9781003221876-6

information with the formation of novel, non-intuitive connections; remembering and stabilizing memories not yet consolidated, as well as forgetting.

Psychoanalysis, the cognitive sciences, and neurophysiology describe dream activity according to their investigation specificities, which can be summarized as follows:

—the subjectivity of the dream in relation to its contents,
—the cognitive functions involved,
—the underlying neuronal scaffolding.

Therefore, neurophysiology describes the organization of sleep through its circuits, the brain structures involved, the electrical organization and neuroimaging, while the other two disciplines, more broadly, share the research on its functions. The search for the meaning of dreams and their interpretation within an analytical framework are, instead, almost exclusive to psychoanalysis.

All this suggests that dreaming, and therefore the experience of sleep and the (almost) ubiquitous activity of dreaming in the animal kingdom, can be analyzed from many different perspectives. We will take into consideration some views that are relevant, according to us, to frame dreams back into psychotherapeutic work.

From a conventional linguistic point of view, wakefulness and sleeping are a classic duality. This duality is marked by the presence or absence of consciousness.

> Conscious experience during sleep (i.e. dreaming) has classically been considered a phenomenon entirely distinct from the spontaneous thought and imagery of wakefulness. But to the contrary, emerging evidence suggests that dream experiences may best be conceptualized as a natural extension of waking consciousness, overlapping in both phenomenology and neural mechanism (Wamsley & Stickgold, 2010; Domhoff, 2011; Horikawa et al., 2013). In both resting wakefulness and sleep, the mind/brain is hard at work processing the day's events and concerns—consolidating memory (Plihal & Born, 1997; Mednick et al., 2002; Tucker et al., 2006), integrating new information with our existing knowledge (Tamminen et al., 2010; Lewis and Durrant, 2011), and perhaps even using past experience to plan for the future (Wilhelm et al., 2011).
>
> (Wamsley, 2013, p. 1)

What remains of waking, and is revealed in the dream, is a particular state of consciousness in which there is always a minimal phenomenal selfhood experience (Windt, 2015a) that does not fade even during deep sleep (Thompson, 2015).

In fact, upon awakening, even if we are not aware (for a few moments) of where we are, with whom, and how we got there:

We do not have to turn around to see who it was who was just asleep and unknowing, if by 'who' we mean the sense of self as the embodied subject of present-moment experience in contrast to the sense of self as the mentally represented object of autobiographical memory. This intimate and immediate bodily self-awareness that we have as we emerge from sleep into waking life suggests that there may be some kind of deep-sleep awareness.

(Thompson, 2015, p. 1)

That is, even in the deepest sleep, a minimal consciousness of the Self persists, which is not lost even in the simplest dream or, according to the author, in the dreamless sleep.

Dream consciousness

The dream is a specific state of consciousness activated within a system closed to external stimulations, therefore without environmental stimuli to respond to.

It is a state in which the subjective experience completely depends on the internal environment. This is strongly suggested by the data. The brain shows global activity, which can be measured by the degree of temporal coordination of different networks and regions to the overall mean of its activity. Measuring the brain's global activity is like measuring the degree of noise and speech each person produces within a group, relative to the overall group noise. If one person shouts louder, she/he will dominate, but may still be less aligned with the overall group as a person who does not speak at all. The person best synchronized with the rest of the group is the one who produces the same degree of noise and speech as the overall mean or average of all persons together, i.e. the group.

Why may a brain be different from persons and groups?

What the person is to the group, so are the individual regions or networks to the overall mean activity of the brain, that is, to its overall activity. And in the same way, a person may be more or less timewise synchronized with the group as a whole, and regions or networks may be more or less strongly synchronized with the brain's mean overall activity. Usually, in the wakefulness state, there is a balance between regions–networks related to internally oriented cognition like the Self and those involved more in externally oriented cognition like the external environment, i.e. non-self. One can say the balance is 50/50, half Self, half environment.

According to Tanabe et al. (2020), this 50/50 balance changes during sleep. Regions and networks involved in externally oriented cognition, like sensory regions, and the attention network, are now decoupled from the brain's mean overall activity; they are desynchronized from the brain's global activity and hence no longer have any impact, just like a person who is not talking at all has no impact on the group. In the same way, the internally oriented regions and networks have a greater impact on sleep since they are more synchronized with the brain's global activity (Tanabe et al., 2020)—the 50/50 balance in the awake state thus shifts to, let's say, an 80/20 balance in sleep. In other terms, the Self takes over in sleep and has a much stronger impact on the brain's global activity with respect to the external environment; that is why dreams during sleep are so much focused upon the Self.

While sleeping, according to Kozmová (2012): 'Occurrence, quality, intensity, and extent of specific mental faculties' could oscillate, remain the same, or change according to alterations in a particular state of consciousness' (p. 47).

The dream maintains its form of primary consciousness associated with an impoverishment of language skills or, in any case, with all secondary and tertiary functions, such as abstract thinking, volition, metacognition, and so on (D'Agostino et al., 2013).

The biggest difference with respect to wakefulness is the absence of self-reflective awareness, which makes it possible to distinguish between reality and the internal production of images, fantasies, and dreams. In fact, it is only upon awakening that we realize that we were dreaming; while dreaming, this awareness vanishes. The exception to this distinction is lucid dreams also belonging to the resting state. Like our mental faculties and their different layers such as wakeful awareness, dreaming non-awareness, and lucid dreaming awareness, the brain's spontaneous activity too may develop along different time and space dynamic layers. It is still unclear how many layers the spontaneous activity features, and how they differ in terms of time and space patterns. It is clear is that the brain's neural activity exhibits a complex hierarchy with different temporospatial dynamic layers; how these translate into the various mental hierarchy layers is uncharted territory, at least for now.

Voss et al. (2014) found that:

> Below the sensory threshold, stimulation with 25 and 40 Hz was able to induce secondary consciousness in dreams. The effect was not observed for lower or higher frequencies, suggesting that the rate and/or periodicity of oscillatory activity in the brain is causally relevant for higher cognitive functioning and that lower gamma-band activity may indeed be a necessary condition for the elicitation of secondary consciousness in dreams, perhaps even in waking.
>
> (Voss et al., 2014, p. 812)

According to these authors, in lucid dreams, secondary consciousness elements coexist with the of primary consciousness ones present in the REM phase.

Therefore, consciousness can no longer be considered as the foundation of the wake–sleep dichotomy, and nor can the NON-REM–REM phases in dreams. New evidence clearly shows that dreaming occurs in all phases of sleep:

Many experimental studies have shown oneiric mental production in Sleep Onset (SO), Stage 2 (St.2) and Slow Wave Sleep (SWS), which is not predicted by the REM/NREM sleep dichotomy. Furthermore, experimental data support the hypothesis that cognitive processes involved in dream generation could be the same in the different sleep stages.

(Occhionero et al., 2005, p. 77)

In their survey on the presence of high-order cognitive (HOC) skills in dreaming, Kahan and LaBerge (2011) concede that the dreaming mind is highly similar to the waking mind. Based on two experiments designed to find similarities and differences in cognition, as well as to compare the participants' ratings of the sensory and structural features of their dreaming and waking experiences, they conclude: 'High-order cognition is much more common in dreams than has been assumed, so any theory of dreaming that does not take this into account is out-of-date' (Kahan & LaBerge, 2011, p. 509).

Now evidence shows that the continuity theory holds not only for the similarities of mental content throughout states, but also for similarities at the process levels of cognition (Kahan & LaBerge, 2011).

The dream Self

What has just been described clearly shows that sleep/dream represents a particular state of consciousness in which the dreamer is detached and unaware of what surrounds him, but, at the same time, he is completely immersed in an imaginary reality characterized by the same elements of wakefulness. An imaginary reality he knows nothing about until he wakes up.

This is the only physiological, spontaneously recurring state in which complex subjective experiences depend almost exclusively on information stored within the brain. For this reason, dreaming is said to reveal consciousness itself 'in a very special, pure, and isolated form (Revonsuo, 2006).

(D'Agostino et al., 2013, p. 2)

If the structure of cognitive processes in sleep/dream does not differ much from the structure of waking, i.e. if we can ascribe to the dream, albeit partially, the use of the same thought processes of waking, what seems to be differently reproduced in the dream is the structure of the Self, both with respect to waking and in the various stages of sleep.

While the dream Self appears to be impoverished in its access to systems like autobiographical memories, bodily awareness, self-monitoring and that form of consciousness that yields a unity of experience that the Self 'owns', the dream Self appears to surpass the waking Self with respect to the experience of emotions and perceptiveness.

(McNamara, 2007, p. 114)

These qualitative differences of the representation of the Self, and of memories in sleep/dream, compared to the waking state, give us interesting clues about mental functioning in the absence of environmental stimuli (externally oriented cognitive tasks), therefore also outside the analytical setting.

Certainly, the Self that appears in the narrated dream will not accurately reflect the Self present in the dream (NON-REM or REM), but, due to its constant presence in the dream activity, it can be considered a test case of the transformative processes of mental activity.

McNamara (2007) describes some functions of the Self in the wakeful state:

Cognitive neuroscientific studies of the Self indicate that virtually every higher cognitive function is influenced by the Self: memories are encoded more efficiently when referred to the Self (Kelly et al., 2002; Fink et al., 1996; Craik, Moroz, & Moscovitch, 1999), feelings and affective responses always include the Self (Davidson, 2001; LeDoux, 2002), fundamental attributions of intentionality, agency, and mind all concern Selves in interaction with other Selves (Gallagher, 2000; Vogeley & Fink, 2003) and so on.

(McNamara, 2007, p. 113)

And in the dream:

Interestingly, all of the above properties of the Self are notably altered in the dreaming Self—the 'I' that dreams. Although we experience ourselves as a 'Self' when we dream, the Self in many dreams cannot be said to exhibit normal access to autobiographical memory, normal emotional reactions, or any of the other standard phenomenological properties of the waking Self mentioned above.

(McNamara, 2007, p. 114)

So, what do we find of the Self in the dream?

Therefore, even in the simplest forms of dreams, that is dreams with poorly retrievable images or sounds, even in these scanty memories, there is always the sensation of 'being' present in the dream or at least of 'having' a Self. It is not a Self that can be considered as the duplicate of the wakeful activity (Windt, 2015b), hence a Self with the complex characteristics described in the previous chapters.

What is described as a 'dreaming Self' on awakening is characterized by the 'I' (the dreaming Self—the 'I' that dreams. McNamara (2007), located somewhere in the dream present moment. This 'I' can be personified by ourselves, or placed in other people, animals, or objects.

The quality of the dream experience can also be equal to the quality of the wakeful experience (Revonsuo, 2006), but, as we have seen, it does not feature the quality of the space–time continuity that the Self has in the wakeful state, the form of self-reflective thinking, autobiographical coherence and often not even the fact of having a body. So, self-awareness and reflectiveness in dreams are not comparable with the richness and fullness of wakefulness; but, despite all this, the dreaming Self is totally immersed in the reality of the dream, by 'being there' in the 'here and now' of the dream, with all its figurative and metaphorical richness.

The 'here and now' of the dream

Let us investigate the 'here and now' of the dream.

The presence of the Self in the dream is a space–time construction; that is the Self is located in a space represented by the dream (here) and character-ized by a present time (now) that proceed together or separately.

> Even though this sense of identification with a phenomenal here and now in involves a drastically reduced form of phenomenal selfhood, it is still sufficient to ground retrospective claims of having had a self in dream reports. The basic structural feature of a self that is experienced as dis-tinct from and located at a precise point within the world is preserved. To be sure, the locus of self-location and self-identification is more fluid in dreams than in wakefulness.
>
> (Windt, 2015a, p. 16)

This reduced form of phenomenal selfhood, which the author calls the 'minimal form of phenomenal selfhood' (Windt, 2015a), is always present in the dream and can be traced back in the dream content, even when it seems to be devoid of space–time references. When even the 'now' of the dream is lost, or it seems vague and indefinite, i.e. when through the 'now' a specific self-location cannot be identified, the subjectivity of the dream remains alive and so does that of the dreamer experiencing the dream as 'pure subjective temporality' (Windt, 2015a), which 'is a candidate for minimal phenomenal experience; it is a condition for but still more basic than minimal phenomenal selfhood' (Windt, 2015a, p. 17).

The dreamer who experiences the dream (I had a dream, I dreamed of) still brings his subjective experience of having experienced the existence of the Self even without images to remember/recount. A minimal unreal and dis-embodied Self, not controlled by the wakeful thought processes, anarchic and bizarre but deeply related to and identified with the dreamer.

We can reject the object of identification of the Self in the dream (it wasn't me; it was …), but we cannot reject 'being' the subject who had that dream. In the dream, 'being' and the 'Self' coincide with their space–time structure and the present (here and now) is the time of the dream.

What do we mean by time and space in dreams? We all know the famous clock painted by Salvador Dali, based on his experience during his dreams; he used to take short naps with an intense dream experience, which, as soon as he woke up due to noise, he immediately wrote down and sketched. Time and space are experienced in an abnormal way in dreams; for instance, it is possible to suddenly experience the Self in incredibly fast time speeds and space extensions you would usually only dream of in the wakeful state.

Where are such temporospatial distortions in our Self's experience during dreams coming from? The brain is to blame. As noted throughout this book, the brain's temporospatial dynamic is central for mental features and therefore also for dreams. During dreams, the temporospatial dynamic can 'do whatever it wants' as it is decoupled from any external constraints; that's why it goes 'awry' and may result in hitherto unknown speeds and extensions in dreams.

Sleep and memory

The dream speaks in the present, while incorporating traces (episodes, objects, environments) of the past.

This present time, which we find in the 'here and now' of the dream, maintains the illusion of the First-Person Perspective and therefore of its subjectivity. Through the present continuous, the scenes of the dream are set in the present. That is, through the total immersion of the Self in the imaginary reality of the dream, the Self, agent and observer of the dream, lives through the flow of images unfolding as they are being created.

The present is the time of the dream, which is produced by integrating daytime residues:

> Once the daytime residues (emotions, thoughts, and concerns we are not always aware of) have been incorporated into the dream, they start to dance from one cerebral area (Zellner, 2013) to the other, getting rid of some elements (sensory de-afferentation and inhibition of the executive functions), being enriched by others, creating new links from memory fragments (Payne & Nadel, 2004; Schredl, 2010) speaking in the present while recruiting old memories, and in the end, they turn up transformed and impossible to recognize when remembering the dream.
>
> (Spagnolo, 2018, p.13)

So, sleep/dream is an interactive process through brain structures actively communicating and creating new scenarios.

The sleep/dream process breaks up, patches up, erases, and stabilizes memories. In what way?

Recent studies (Langille, 2019; Todorova & Zugaro, 2019) show that, during sleep, the cortex and the hippocampus actively talk and the resulting reorganization leads to the stabilization of memories.

Todorova and Zugaro (2019) have shown that, during slow sleep, the hippocampus spontaneously fires up and selectively sends information to the neocortex, which in turn responds by activating itself. This specific exchange of information is often followed by a period of silence (delta waves) and then by the typical rhythmic activity of sleep through 'sleep spindles'. According to the authors, this intense exchange plays an important role in memory consolidation. Instead, it is not clear why there is a period of silence after the exchange of information between the hippocampus and the cortex.

We know that new information is stored in different types of memories. Neuroscientists call this the multiple memory systems (Poldrack & Packard, 2003), and have proposed a dual-memory theory (Squire & Dede, 2015): hippocampus-dependent and non-hippocampus-dependent, or simply, declarative and non-declarative (procedural) memory. Moreover, the hippocampus and the neocortex are the neural structures associated with the temporary and long-term memory stores, respectively.

New information is simultaneously encoded in both memory stores. In his introduction, Langille (2019) suggests:

> Current memory models maintain that these two brain structures accomplish unique, but interactive, memory functions. Specifically: most modeling suggests that memories are rapidly acquired during the waking experience by the hippocampus, before being later consolidated into the cortex for long-term storage. Sleep has been shown to be critical for the transfer and consolidation of memories in the cortex.
>
> (p. 1)

During subsequent consolidation periods, it is assumed that this network will make it possible to strengthen and integrate new memories with pre-existing memories in a long-term memory store. Offline periods, such as sleep (Rasch & Born, 2013), are considered as ideal for reproduction, since no new incoming information will interfere with consolidation.

The studies of Todorova and Zugaro (2019) also show that, while sleeping, it is the hippocampus that dictates which cortical neurons will remain active during the exchange between the two brain structures. It seems that it is precisely this link between the hippocampus and the neocortex that manages the consolidation (and the cancellation) of memories. In fact, in this stabilization process, an important role is assigned to the possibility of erasing memories. If whatever is encoded during the days is not regularly cleared, the brain circuits would soon be saturated and unable to retain new information (Langille, 2019).

Let us try to simplify the rather complex interaction among brain structures:

> Memories are remembered during NREM (SPW) and REM (theta) sleep for two reasons operating in anti-parallel: first, to consolidate recently encoded information at the systems and/or synaptic level—perhaps

through a mechanism where NREMS lays down and edits an unstable cortical trace which is then stabilized and integrated by REMS—and second, to gradually erase hippocampal memory traces as the information represented by these traces is consolidated to stable neocortical storage. Additional oscillations act to fine-tune the brains memory bank during sleep by interacting with ripples to stabilize adaptive information (signal) and by acting in isolation to remove irrelevant, non-adaptive data (noise).

(Langille, 2019, p. 15)

We are completely unaware of all this continuous exchange both in NON-REM and REM phases, since it happens 'offline'. We retain only some few fragments caught in the memory of a dream. For this reason, the analysis of the content of dreams is the only way to enter this reality (sleep) in which we plunge every day and which we would be totally unaware of without remembering our dreams.

Dream production

Saying that sleep is actively involved in manipulating memory traces and dreaming is present in all phases of sleep does not mean that whatever happens offline at night is a replica of what happens when we are online, when awake. According to Hartmann (2007), dreams do not reproduce daytime material, but they change it, recombine it, and weave it to build ongoing stories; in other words, dreams show a broader and looser hyperconnectivity with respect to wakefulness. Dreams can be compared to an artistic creation, capable of recombining past elements to create new shapes. According to this author, the creation of an artistic work is supported by what is emotionally significant for the artist; in the same way, it is possible to think of dreaming in terms of its ability to generate new connections by emotions. Hartmann (2007) suggests that, although there is no convincing empirical evidence on emotional integration as a function of the dream, following the dream production of a patient, for a long time, it is possible to see this process of integration and transformation at work. Therefore, starting from the assumption that the dream is a form of mental functioning, he places it at one of the poles of a wake-sleep continuum, which unfolds between focused waking thought at one end, through reverie, daydreaming, and fantasy to dreaming at the other end.

Its hyperconnectivity always involves new connections and new creations, which do not happen randomly, but they are guided by the dreamer's emotions or at least by his concerns. The stronger and more significant the worry/emotion, the more powerful the central image sustaining the dream. This image is linked to the metaphorical language used by the dream, not for its figurative capacity, but because it is placed at one of the two poles of the wake-sleep continuum, with logical, serial thought bound to the rules of verbal language at the other extreme.

Therefore, as a creative recombination of memory and knowledge, the dream is significantly related to what was described before about memory storage and about what it means to evoke them. But before dwelling on this last point, we would like to devote some more time to dreams and memory. It is possible to place the autobiographical memory within the declarative framework as a set of experiences, information, memories, both episodic (EMs) and semantic, all linked to the development of the Self. Horton and Malinowski (2015) analyze memory consolidation processes during sleep, paying special attention to the improvement, stabilization, and integration of autobiographical memory (AMs). In describing this process, they use the concept of hyperassociativity underlying dream production. Autobiographical memories are broken down into their constitutive fragments, reactivated during sleep and hyperassociated into a new dream experience. In this way, sleep can also improve autobiographical memories because this recasting leads to retrieve and consolidate the salient elements of memories through their repetition in the dream.

> The function of this could be to allow specific fragments of waking experiences to be selectively reproduced, perhaps played out in a novel or bizarre context, rendering them context-free and subsequently increasing their inter-relations with other, more loosely-associated memory fragments. EMs, which are by definition context bound, engage hippocampal regions. AMs, instead, can be context-free and the advantage of this over time is that previously learned information is easily retrieved in any context, facilitating accessibility.
>
> (Horton & Malinowski, 2015, p. 4)

The concept of Self-consolidation (Horton et al., 2009) can be likened to the recombination of the elements of autobiographical memory, which is decontextualized and therefore available for new links, and to the inclusion of these fragments in new sequences, in the frame of the above-mentioned 'here and now', i.e. in the space–time continuity that is, in the frame of the space–time continuity of the subjectivized and subjectivizing Self of the dream. The meaning provided by Horton et al. (2009) is linked to the integration of goals and recent experience, represented by self-images such as 'I am', while we believe that all the sleep/dreamwork is designed to give strength to the space–time structure of the Self, through which we experience continuity and subjectivity (minimal selfhood experience) and, more broadly, as described by Fosshage (2013):

> Dreaming is thinking when we are asleep. By definition, dreaming is unconscious thinking, and I see it as the continuation of implicit and explicit processing that occurs during waking. It offers the best window into unconscious thinking. And what do we dream about? We dream

about our most immediate concerns: our dreams include attempts to resolve conflict, to self-regulate, to regulate affect, to envision and move developmentally, to fortress threatened patterns of organization, to consolidate new experience, and to integrate and enhance new learning.

(Fosshage, 2013, p. 253)

Dream narrative

What has been described in the previous paragraphs may suggest that it is precisely the re-enactment, the ability to remember some fragments of a dream, which offers the possibility of looking beyond the window of wakeful consciousness, to understand what happens to the structure of the Self, and more broadly, to the inner world of the patient.

'Dreams are never occupied with minor details', wrote Freud (1900, p. 586).

In this sense, the mental activity present during sleep is just as important as that of wakefulness. Moreover, while in the wakeful consciousness certain elements appear as a synthesis (linked to the attentional and executive system), in the dream, where there is no need for an executive output (restful state, or in general no active, performative, tasks), everything may coexist and be simultaneously figurative. Bizarre elements, paradoxes, hypersensory deployments and intense emotional reactions negotiate their way into the dream consciousness by virtue of the loose link with the prefrontal critical functions. Blechner (2005) speaks about the 'grammar of irrationality'. This 'irrationality', which is different from 'bizarreness', is experienced by every dreamer and involves two dream phenomena, called by this author: disjunctive and interobject cognitions. Bizarreness in the dream is very frequent and:

> In the sciences of dreaming, the 'bizarreness' of dream reports is often analyzed into three distinct forms. The most common form of bizarreness is incongruity or mismatch of character, event, or setting, followed by vagueness or uncertainty, while full-scale discontinuity of narrative sequence is the least common.
>
> (Rosen & Sutton, 2013, p. 1042)

These unrealistic, bizarre, irrational elements are not isomorphic with reality; they attract the attention of the dreamer, and of the researcher, because they go beyond the common sense of the iconic representation. In addition, through the oneiric representation, they conjure up all the emotional intensity of the strongly invested events. Presentification in the dream represents the time dimension of dream consciousness where, apparently, there is no memory of the events, even though they do happen in the present; an interesting difference with respect to wakeful thought that is continuously in contact with the past and is projected to the future. 'So, the dream may be considered as a kind of bridge between areas of the mind not always connected during waking' (Castellet Y Ballarà et al., 2019, p. 49) and it may be considered not as 'the royal road' to the unconscious but to self-awareness; including in self-awareness the insight, i.e. the moment when an intrapsychic fact, or an embodied memory, becomes emotionally real, i.e. undeniable and meaningful (Castellet Y Ballarà et al., 2019).

Dream and treatment

The current interest of psychoanalysis in understanding sleep is not all direc-ted at decoding symbols or to enucleating the meaning of its underlying latent content from its manifest content, but to have information about the patient's inner world, about the structure of the Self, about affective relationships, and above all about the transformations during psychotherapy.

Therefore, it is not the single dream, detached from the therapist–patient relational context, which provides the essential information for the therapy, but the whole contextual sequence in which it is framed. Here context means the material and transferential relationship with the patient, the reality of the setting and of daily events as well as the patient's biography and pathobio-graphy, in a few words the ecology of the mind. We are interested in dreams, and we are going to describe some of them related to the clinical cases pre-sented because, according to Blechner (2013), they help to:

—regulate mood (Kramer, 1993);
—make connections between dissociated areas of awareness 'in a safe place', and thus perform a kind of psychotherapy (Hartmann, 1995);
—formulate 'extra-linguistic thoughts' that could not be formulated in waking thinking (Blechner, 1998);
—create 'thought mutations' as an oneiric Darwinism, i.e. new ideas and objects, created through partially random processes, that the mind can then retain if useful or reject if useless (Blechner, 2001).

In his work on the role of dreams in evolution Franklin (2005) concludes: 'The processing of dream content, which consists of variations in scenarios encountered during daily life in which we interact with the physical and social world, is bound to influence our cognitive capacities and subsequent appraisal of real-world content' (p. 74).

In the next chapter, we will explore the transformations of the Self during treatment.

References

Blechner, M. (1998). The analysis and creation of dream meaning: Interpersonal, intrapsychic, and neurobiological perspectives. *Contemporary Psychoanalysis*, 34:181–194.

Blechner, M. (2001). *The dream frontier*. Hillsdale: Analytic Press.

Blechner, M.J. (2005). The grammar of irrationality. *Contemporary Psychoanalysis*, 41:203–221.

Blechner, M.J. (2013). New ways of conceptualizing and working with dreams. *Contemporary Psychoanalysis*, 49(2):259–275.

Castellet, Y., Ballarà, F., Spadazzi, C., & Spagnolo, R. (2019). Il sogno tra neuroscienze e psicoanalisi. *Psicobiettivo*, 39(2):33–56.

Craik, F. I. M., Moroz, T. M., Moscovitch, M. (1999). In search of the self: A positron emission tomography study. *Psychological Science*, 10:129–178.

D'Agostino, A., Castelnovo, A., & Scarone, S. (2013). Dreaming and the neurobiology of self: recent advances and implications for psychiatry. *Frontiers Psychology*, 4 (680):1–4.

Davidson, R. J. (2001). Toward a biology of personality and emotion. *Annals of the New York Academy of Sciences*, 935:191–207.

Domhoff, W. (2011). The neural substrate for dreaming: Is it a subsystem of the default network? *Consciousness and Cognition*, 20(4):1163–1174.

Fink, G. R., Markowitsch, H. J., Reinkemeier, M., Bruckbauer, T., Kessler, J., Heiss, W. D. (1996). Cerebral representation of one's own past: Neural networks involved in autobiographical memory. *Journal of Neuroscience*, 16:4275–4282.

Fosshage, J. (2013). The dream narrative. *Contemporary Psychoanalysis*, 49(2):253–258.

Franklin, M.S. (2005). The role of dreams in the evolution of the human mind. *Evolutionary Psychology*, 3: 59–78.

Freud, S. (1900). *The interpretations of dreams*. S.E., 4–5. London: Hogarth.

Gallagher, S. (2000). Philosophical conceptions of the self: Implications for cognitive science. *Trends in Cognitive Sciences*, 4:14–21.

Hartmann, E. (1995). Making connections in a safe place: Is dreaming psychotherapy? *Dreaming*, 5: 213–228.

Hartmann, E. (2007). The nature and functions of dreaming. In: D. Barrett & P. McNamara (Eds), *The new science of dreaming* (pp.171–192). Westport: Praeger.

Horikawa, T., Tamaki, M., Miyawaki, Y., and Kamitani, Y. (2013). Neural decoding of visual imagery during sleep. *Science*, 340: 639–642. doi:10.1126/science.1234330

Horton, C.L., Moulin, C.J.A., & Conway, M.A. (2009). The self and dreams during a period of transition. *Consciousness and Cognition*, 18(3):710–717.

Horton, C.L., & Malinowski, J.E. (2015). Autobiographical memory and hyperassociativity in the dreaming brain: implications for memory consolidation in sleep. *Frontiers Psychology*, 6(874):1–14.

Kahan, T. L., & LaBerge, S.P. (2011). Dreaming and waking: Similarities and differences revisited. *Consciousness and Cognition*, 20: 494–514.

Kelley, W. M., Macrae, C. N., Wayland, C. L., Caglar, S., Inati, S., Heatherton, T. F. (2002). Finding the self? An event related fMRI study. *Journal of Cognitive Neuroscience*, 14:785–794.

Kozmová, M. (2012). Dreamers as agents making strategizing efforts exemplify core aggregate of executive function in non-lucid dreaming. *International Journal of Dream Research*, 5(1):47–67.

Kramer, M. (1993). The selective mood regulatory function of dreaming: An update and revision. In A. Moffitt, M. Kramer, & R. Hoffmann (Eds), *The functions of dreaming* (pp. 139–195). Albany: State University of New York Press.

Langille, J. J. (2019). Remembering to forget: a dual role for sleep oscillations in memory consolidation and forgetting. *Frontiers Cellular Neuroscience*, 13(71): 1–21.

LeDoux, J. E. (2002). *Synaptic self: How our brains become who we are*. New York: Viking.

McNamara, P. (2007). Representation of the Self in REM and NREM Dreams. *Dreaming*, 17(2): 113–126.

McNamara, P. (2011). *The appearance and role of the self in dreams*. https://www.psycholo gytoday.com/ie/blog/dream-catcher/201107/the-appearance-and-role-the-self-in-dreams.

Occhionero, M., Cicogna, P., Natale, V., Esposito, M. J., & Bosinelli, M. (2005). Representation of self in SWS and REM Dreams. *Sleep and Hypnosis*, 7(2): 77–83.

Payne, J. & Nadel, L. (2004). Sleep, dreams, and memory consolidation: The role of the stress hormone cortisol. *Learning Memory*, 11:671–678. doi:1072-0502/04

Poldrack, R. A., & Packard, M. G. (2003). Competition among multiple memory systems: Converging evidence from animal and human brain studies. *Neuropsychologia*, 41(3):245–251.

Rasch, B., & Born, J. (2013). About sleep's role in memory. *Physiological Reviews*, 93(2): 681–766.

Revonsuo, A. (2006). *Inner presence: Consciousness as a biological phenomenon*. Cambridge, MA: MIT Press.

Rosen, M., & Sutton, J. (2013). Self-Representation and perspectives in dreams. *Philosophy Compass*, 8(11): 1041–1053.

Schredel, M. (2010). Characteristics and content in dream. *International Review of Neurobiology*, 92:135–154.

Spagnolo, R. (2018). *Building Bridges. The impact of Neuropsychoanalysis on psychoanalytic clinical session*. London/New York: Routledge.

Squire, L.R., & Dede, A.J.O. (2015). Conscious and unconscious memory systems. *Cold Spring Harbor Perspectives in Biology*, 7:1–14.

Tanabe, S., Huang, Z., Zhang, J., Chen, Y., Fogel, S., Doyon, J., Wu, J., Xu, J., Zhang, J., Qin, P., Wu, X., Mao, Y., Mashour, G.A., Hudetz, A.G., & Northoff, G. (2020). Altered global brain signal during physiologic, pharmacologic, and pathologic states of unconsciousness in humans and rats. *Anesthesiology*, 132(6):1392–1406. doi:10.1097/ALN.0000000000003197.

Thompson, E. (2015). Dreamless sleep, the embodied mind, and consciousness. In T. Metzinger & J. M. Windt (Eds), *Open MIND*: 37(T). Frankfurt am Main: MIND Group.

Todorova, R., & Zugaro, M. (2019). Isolated cortical computations during delta waves support memory consolidation. *Science*, 366 (6463): 377–381.

Vogeley, K., & Fink, G. R. (2003). Neural correlates of the first-person perspective. *Trends in Cognitive Sciences*, 7:38–42.

Voss, U., Holzmann, R., Hobson, A., Paulus, W., Koppehele-Gossel, J., Klimke, A., & Nitsche. A.M. (2014). Induction of self-awareness in dreams through frontal low current stimulation of gamma activity. *Nature Neuroscience*, 17(6):810–814.

Wamsley, E. J., and Stickgold, R. (2010). Dreaming and offline memory processing. *Current Biology*, 20: R1010–R1013. doi:10.1016/j.cub.2010.10.045.

Wamsley, E.J. (2013). Dreaming, waking, conscious experience, and the resting brain: Report of subjective experience as a tool in the cognitive neurosciences. *Frontiers in Psychology*, 4(637):1–7.

Windt, J. M. (2015a). Just in time—dreamless sleep experience as pure subjective temporality—a commentary on Evan Thompson. In T. Metzinger & J. M. Windt (Eds), *Open MIND*:37(C). Frankfurt am Main: MIND Group.

Windt, J. M. (2015b). *Dreaming: a conceptual framework for philosophy of mind and empirical research*. Cambridge/London: MIT Press.

Zellner, M. (2013). Dreaming and the default mode network. *Contemporary Psychoanalysis*, 49(2):226–2032.

Chapter 6

Dream experience of the Self

CX: The working through with recurrent dreams

In the previous chapters, we have described the evolution of several clinical cases. In some of these cases, we have illustrated the patients' dreams within the analytical setting, which spontaneously accompany the working through during the session. In this chapter, we will add some more clinical elements to the analysis of the dreams during therapy.

We return to Chapter 3, to patient CX, and to one of her recurring dreams.

CX has had the same recurring dream for years: she has to leave and has to pack, but she has more and more stuff to put in her luggage, and no room for all the clothes. The more she packs, the fuller the room becomes with clothes waiting to be packed. She misses the train (or plane) because she can't close her luggage.

This dream came out many times during the psychotherapy before the stage of her compulsive use of Fb.

In the first phase of the therapy, the psychotherapist and the patient focused on her anxiety over not being able to leave, which always accompanied the dream, on the missed appointments, and the underachievement she experienced in her life. It seemed *as if* she could never finish anything. *As if* there was something unfinished waiting to be done. So, the analysis of the dream was designed to control and manage her anxiety. The work on the dream was linked to emotions and their homeostasis. No association was made about the incompleteness of the Self and its lack of attunement.

As her anxiety diminished, the dream work shifted to the structure and the flow of her thought: the patient was unable to process all these thoughts; they were far too many; they always filled her head and escaped any containment. Being overwhelmed with thoughts left her confused and unable to choose. The onset of the patient's obsessive thought and compulsive use of Fb revealed what the dream had figuratively shown for a long time, that is, that one thought was pulling another thought and then another, until they filled her head, or the suitcase and the room (including the analytical setting), without being able to discriminate what to keep and what to discard (delete).

DOI: 10.4324/9781003221876-7

In the second part of the therapy, after revealing she had lived in a community, during the work on the restructuring of her Self, the dream seemed to indicate something else. Her container-Self was too small to hold all that stuff. The Self could not mobilize many resources to meet all the demands coming from her surroundings. She apparently did not own all the things that were in the room; a lot of stuff belonged to the community; she was not able to integrate it and so it remained out of her suitcase, piled up, stacked, without knowing what to do with it. Moreover, having mixed up everything in the same suitcase, she was unable to recognize which objects belonged to her and which ones belonged to the community. What was subjective and what was objective.

The same sensations were constantly present in the psychotherapist's countertransference.

She perceived that the spaces of the Self were not well distributed (something too small, the suitcase, it should have contained something larger, the room, which was inside many other rooms), and became large and narrow out of all proportion; and, above all, she perceived that time was sometimes too short and felt pressured (*the train is about to leave, the plane is about to take off and I can't make it ... I have to hurry*). Sometimes it expanded out of all proportion, in the slow gestures of filling the suitcase, through an endless action. So, this dream (along with others) conjures up the figure of a matryoshka Self that contains the selves of the whole community. We have empty it very slowly to reach its smallest structure and start from it again.

At the end of the analysis, this recurring dream is transformed: there are many suitcases of different sizes, she can selectively make room for all her stuff, and she can choose what to put in her luggage according to her journey and which suitcase to use. The Self evolves like the dream; it shifts from confusion and chaos, almost split into multiple elements, or bound to the outer space by multiple virtual images, and it acquires an affective, cognitive, relational essence, more able to express needs and desires. Gradually the patient finds her rhythm and learns to respect her time. At times, she is in distress due to the demands coming from her surroundings; other times, she is ready and determined, showing a good mobilization of resources. She learns not to collude with requests by passively accepting them and metaphorically stacking everything without ever integrating anything. She chooses according to her emotional and affective possibilities and to her relational skills. She chooses to change job to be more in tune with her values, thus experiencing more suitable social relationships for her personality. This patient showed all her cognitive and emotional richness also through dreams.

The last dream in the session is about a plane trip where she can bring only one suitcase. She is able to choose the suitcase of the required size, fill it with what is necessary, catch the plane on time and arrive at her destination.

Dreams are not about cognition

Finally, her analytic journey, and the journey to complete her Self, come to fruition.

What happens here? Dreams are not about cognition. Cognition is somewhat shifted into the background during dreams, with no conscious voluntary control over the contents of dreams. This brings up a deeper level of our mental life, beneath the cognitive level, that is bound to specific contents. That deeper level is the dynamic level which dynamic psychotherapists only know too well. That deeper level is no longer characterized by specific content but by an intrinsic temporospatial dynamic over which we have no cognitive control. That deeper dynamic level hosts our Self and is mediated by the spontaneous activity's temporospatial structure.

Recent studies by Wolff et al. (2019) and Huang et al. (2016) demonstrated that, on a psychological level, self-consciousness is closely linked to and predicted by the brain's temporal (and spatial) structure (which can be measured by a scale-free activity and an autocorrelation window). This very same structure features, for instance, various slower and faster frequencies nested within one another like Russian dolls. This temporal structure may be blocked, resulting in less continuity over time and nestedness of the Self; the Self is experienced as being stuck and blocked on one particular time and space scale. A good psychotherapist knows how to liberate the Self from such temporospatial restrictions ... that is what happens when dreams guide and reveal the subjects' true feeling and also provide the royal pathway towards therapeutic improvement as in our case.

We now introduce a patient who was cognitively rigid and with an extremely stiff structure of the Self; she needed another type of work due to her scarce dream production and impoverished mental life.

EX Clinical case: Geometries of the mind

First episode of psychosis: Boom! The brain went boom!

On New Year's Eve, a friend, who is a doctor, requests an urgent consultation for one of his patients who is in the throes of psychomotor agitation, delusions, and hallucinations; she would like to kill her mother. The patient is immediately hospitalized and diagnosed with a first episode of psychosis and discharged about a month later. She is prescribed traditional antipsychotic drugs. She is very subdued. Her prosody is monotonous, her words articulated. She repeats the same words over and over again before starting to speak. She avoids eye contact with facial motor stereotypes and drowsiness. She remembers very little about the days before her hospitalization. Her facial expressions range from sadness to an alert/vigil/persecutory gaze. In these first conversations, she manages to express these thoughts erratically:

I know that I should have died on January 7th, that I should have been calmer in another life … I've already lived this life. I lost everything in the pursuit of a dream, a love that lasted less than a year, an illusion, and then I went haywire. Boom, my brain went boom … I had visions at home; I saw monsters in the backyard; I thought my mother was lying. L. [the friend with whom she was living] *tried to help me, but she couldn't help me … My mum is stronger, so I went back home to my parents. Some scenes aren't visions as they told me (the doctors in the hospital). I already had them in my mind; I felt in danger, I lost all my security. I saw my life flow, and I didn't recognize it… I thought: Boom! The brain went boom! I saw my life flow, and I can't go back now (to live with my mother after leaving home), I thought. My mother was no longer my mother; I thought she was a threat, now she isn't anymore, but she was threatening. She pushed me to work, to be with L.; she wants to buy me a house.*

EX is 40 years old; she arrives at the sessions right on time. Coming in, greeting, starting, and closing the sessions, always following the same pattern. It is like seeing the same scene over and over again in slow motion. When she discontinues her medication, she appears to be more fluid, less awkward; her thought is faster, and the conversation ranges between soliloquy and stereotyped dialogue. She does not recognize herself in what is reported in her medical record; she just remembers that she was very angry at her mother. In addition, she is always reiterating the same narrative linked to her terror of getting ill with infectious diseases (as many as anything she comes in contact with). She slowly manages to talk about herself, about her job as a corporate secretary, about her boyfriend and friends; but she is very detached, as if all this had nothing to do with her. This initial clinical picture is linked to the type of drugs she is taking; when discontinued, she reiterates certain themes, with a slight mood drop, apathy, and clear ideation.

Very slowly, the patient tells about the choice made two years earlier to separate from her mother and go and live in another city with a friend. They were doing many things together, but soon, with this friend, she fell back into the same old drama of her life:

Everyone thinks I am inadequate, incapable of handling anything, almost stupid, that I don't understand anything, and they have to boss me around.

At the same time, she receives two recall letters from her company for mistakes she made. She speaks about this episode a thousand times, always using the same words. When the letter of recall arrives, her mother voices an opinion close to the company's position (according to the patient), saying to her that she should be more careful, better dressed, better groomed, and prettier, since she works in a representative office.

This triggers furious anger in her at the New Year's Eve bouffée; she does not remember the content of this event, only her psychomotor agitation.

From the treatment diary

EX is in psychoanalytic treatment with three sessions a week; she presents with a hyperfixation on ideas, and is always asking the same questions, to which she is always giving the same answers. The exploratory range is narrow: what diseases she may have, whether she can meet her boyfriend or stay in isolation; she wants to go back to work.

The rhythm of the three sessions sometimes allows for pauses through strings of repetitive questions, and answers where it is possible to hook a memory, an emotion, an opinion, something that takes her out of her flat emotional-affective state, which brings her to repeat her soliloquy like a chant. These pauses, and only these brief pauses, bring to light her childhood experience of bodily inadequacy (she was ugly, hairy, poorly groomed, poorly dressed) and intellectual inadequacy (everything had to be explained to her several times). That drove her mother to seek the help of child psychiatrists because she was also mutacic, introverted, and oppository. In these breaks through her monologue, she wants to emphasize that she always felt normal; she was just very angry with her mother, who preferred her more handsome and successful brother (two years younger).

She describes her mother as harsh, cold, formal, not at all sympathetic and never empathic.

At this early stage of the analysis, it is not possible to directly explore the experience of her anger (as it may explode into matricide); so, the psychotherapist slowly begins to propose associations between the characters or the events she recursively speaks about.

Narrative structure

Her narrative follows a very particular approach that can be summed up in this metaphor: it is *as if* she moves from one room to another, and each room contains a plot.

When she is in a room, she talks about events inhabited by certain characters; when she moves into another, she talks about other events with other characters, and so on through three or four rooms at the most. She can also go back and forth in the same room for a long time.

If I interrupt her to introduce a question, a comment, she remains silent and then resumes exactly from where she was interrupted. Sometimes she stops and seems to rewind the speech tape, only to start again by repeating the previous words. She is like a broken LP restarting on its own, but a couple of tracks before. I can even measure the (metaphorical) time and steps it takes to go from one imaginary room to another, all of them on the same horizontal plane.

Her ideation structure is very poor. Her narrative is telegraphic and descriptive. She has little imagination. She can describe entire procedures in detail, but she does not produce a fantasy. If left to her own monologue, she never derails from the ideation tracks on which she travels within the same rooms. In other words, she reveals a rigid and stereotyped structure of the Self, almost with a geometrical scheme.

She describes her childhood life as a formal set of obligations and duties that her mother imposed on her to be socially adequate. In fact, the patient has a very strong sense of duty. She is never late for an appointment. She does exactly what she is required to. She does not tolerate squandering. She never wants anything for herself. She always moves through the same well-known patterns and never puts herself in a different condition.

Over the months, immersed in this exhausting and repetitive narrative of events, I have a mounting feeling that, in front of me, there is a kind of clay giant (she is very tall and stout), who is apparently hard, but easily crushed. And now it seems clearer that the environmental persecution (which triggered the psychotic crisis) was only an opportunity to reinvigorate the ancient splitting nuclei of her Self, tenaciously kept one by one in its own room, which implodes with the anguish of separation and poor social adjustment (*Boom! The brain went boom!*).

Now that I understand this fragility, I become very careful with the tone of my voice (always very soft), with the choice of the words (never negative), with the timing of a small comment, and the respect of her pauses. I almost seem to see the (repetitive and predictable) movements of her thought; I seem to know the geometry of her mind well and so I can follow it step by step.

Slowly she resumes the relationship with her boyfriend and with his family. Her boyfriend is the last born of many siblings; when their mother died their father abandoned them, so they grew up hungry and dejected in the suburbs. Her mother reacts with indignation to this relationship that she considers to be very inappropriate from the social point of view. After 30 sessions, she brings in her first dream:

> I was on a bus with shopping bags. They were full; I was going somewhere, but it was as if I had been kidnapped and I couldn't get off. So, I run away and I find myself at the terminal with lots of buses but I don't know where I am. All the buses are strange to me; I don't feel well; I don't know what to do, where to go. I wake up overwhelmed with anxiety.

I ask her what she was thinking when she woke up, and what she is thinking now. She answers that the whole thing makes her think of tramps because of her grocery bags full of stuff and prone to break. They looked like the ones the homeless carry around with their stuff.

She comes up with an association with her boyfriend's relatives, who almost live like tramps. After many descriptive details about their life, almost an entire session, she adds that she is different from the dream: she has dignity, while they do not. She too moves around a lot by bus, but she is very familiar with all the stops and terminals, she would never get lost. She also wears second-hand clothes, but to save money. Her mum obliges her to save on everything. Nothing is to be squandered. Maybe that is why her bags in her dream were full of groceries, also because she buys food for her boyfriend's whole family and carries it to them by bus. She revisits the dream so many times that in the end she can no longer distinguish between dream, reality, and memories. She gets confused and anxious; she asks if she is crazy, if she is sick, if she does not function, if she is a tramp like M's family. She anxiously asks me what I think of her dream. I conclude by saying:

> *This is the first dream you have brought to the session. It seems important to me you were able to differentiate it from your thoughts and visions. That sometimes makes you feel confused and lost.*

As I recognized the place of the dream (the psychiatric hospital), later on I add that it was important to talk about it (the dream) and share it, because this seems to have restarted her functioning brought to a halt by the hospitalization and by all the drugs she was prescribed.

The dreaming mind

The narrative of her dream gives us a glimpse of functioning, which is sometimes still jammed and confusing. The map of her very familiar and reachable places is not intact; it has holes, jumps that disorient her. Her way of telling and repeating the same things as in a refrain, her jamming and starting again from the previous point, may be a way to find continuity when the thread of thought breaks and the primary functions of the Self are lost (space–time disorientation). The possibility of telling her dream seems to suggest the resumption of her mental functioning through certain steps, such as:

—the shift from her exploding mind (psychotic bouffée) to her dreaming mind;
—the possibility of seeing herself dreaming (minimal Selfhood experience) instead of the opposite situation characterized by delusions and hallucinations (in which she did not recognize herself—alien Self);
—the initial recognition of autobiographical memories (herself moving or performing significant and affective actions) and semantic memories (buses, shopping, maps).

In the following months, we work on the value of visiting her boyfriend's family, so different from hers. It is a warm, chaotic family where there is a lot of sharing and empathy and no-one is ever left alone. Several generations live under the same roof, and affective relationships are very close. None of them has ever studied, regularly worked, complied with the rules of civil coexistence; this makes her feel not judged and therefore accepted.

While we work on the internal, relational, and affective value, another dream comes up about this relationship:

> I'm on a Greek island with my mother, maybe my brother, but there are other people. We are going towards our car when I see a plane circling in the sky and crashing to the ground. Panic strikes. Everyone runs away; we cannot find the car, we run, I don't know where, with our shoes soaked with water.

She immediately says she is happy for having dreamed because this never happens, but she does not know what to add to the dream because when she woke up she was calm, with no anxiety. She adds that there was a lot of panic in the dream, but she didn't feel it. *We had to run, and we ran. It's clear nothing could be found in the midst of running. But then everything was fine.* She does not know what else to add, and she remains silent. So, I tell her:

> Your dream is about a very specific place, a Greek island, in a well-defined period of time, i.e. the summer holidays; maybe all this can be reconnected to something; maybe the dream caught something, inside you, to which it gave value and shape, and you were able to remember the dream.

So, as if my intervention had given her permission to speak, she tells me that three things come to her mind about Greece, the plane, and panic. Perhaps Greece was in her dream because she had been there when she was 20 with her mother and her mother's friends.

> It was a nice trip. We had a good time. Mum and Dad were already separated. I don't remember if my brother was with us. I remember my mum's friends whom we got along with. But the plane is related to the trip I made to England when I was eighteen with my brother to learn English. I didn't want to go there; I didn't care about the study holiday. But my mother wouldn't listen to reason. It had to be done because everybody did it. Panic, I don't know; I've never experienced panic. I don't know what it is.

And she abandons the dream to talk about her usual routine. After 'visiting the usual rooms with big steps', she resumes talking exactly from the beginning of the dream, with the same words, and asks me what I think about the dream. In the meantime, my thought has stopped for a moment on the three associative elements she has brought up; they are at the crossroads of different autobiographical episodes, of different memories, of different periods of Self-development.

The dream provides these elements on a catastrophic substratum that she denies; her associations are descriptive, but devoid of affects. I choose to explore only the denied part, the emotional experience, panic, in order to understand to what extent her affects and representations are split. I choose an exploratory and not an affirmative or assertive mode to avoid introducing hypercritical or persecutory instances. My answer:

> *I don't have much to say about the dream; I was just wondering what cat-astrophic element you had put in the dream through, for example, the crashing plane, or your running away, or, also, your shoes all soaked in water that certainly didn't help you escape.*

Once again, she acts as if I had legitimized her story and continues weaving the narrative by adding that when she was 20, she felt sick. She had diarrhoea for days and days. She pooed in her pants all the time. She was seen by many specialists who found nothing wrong with her and told her it was a psycho-logical reaction. *Maybe you were slowly breaking down*, I tell her; *also, you were scared, and you literally shit yourself.* EX replies:

> *Maybe I wanted to die; it was my way of reacting to the separation of my Mum and Dad. He was right to leave. He had put up with her for too long, do you know what she did? When I was a kid, she was told that if she made us wear orthopaedic shoes, we would get nice feet. And do you know she used to send us to the beach in the summer with our orthopaedic shoes? You know those ugly shoes you buy at the healthcare centres. I was ashamed; I was stifling with sand everywhere. But I couldn't say anything because she had decided it was good for me.*

Even when dreams are telegraphic and adherent to reality, if the work on them is properly done, they mobilize the thought associative ability to sustain the weaving task they elicit.

It is this joint patient–analyst weaving work that makes it possible to draw new scenarios that the patient would not be able to do by herself. With her few cognitive and affective resources, by consistently visiting and revisiting the same rooms, the patient shows she is quite capable of restoring her Self fragmented by the catastrophic anxieties repeatedly haunting her life.

Defence mechanisms

Her defence mechanisms developed to avoid giving in to the psychotic mad-ness of matricide are very strong (obsessiveness, rigidity, compartmentaliza-tion of affects up to the denial of emotions), and bound her Self within a rigid and inflexible temperament structure.

This rigid and inflexible attitude did not fit well with her corporate work because she was 'too zealous'. Her colleagues could no longer stand her after a short period of time, so the company had to repeatedly move her from one room to the other with various tasks, because she was making it difficult for her co-workers to interact with her; in fact, she requires her colleagues to scrupulously comply with all the corporate rules, prohibitions, obligations, etc., as she does. The patient brings all these events as egosyntonic.

Only her relationship with her mother is reportedly dystonic, since she does not realize that she behaves with other employees with her mother's same approach. The more her mother is hypercritical, formal, and demanding in terms of compliance with rules and prohibitions with her, the more she adopts these attitudes *vis-à-vis* her co-workers, identifying herself with the company. It is a split aspect of the Self that identifies itself with her mother/company and that she keeps it separate from other split aspects, such as her relationship with M's family.

In fact, she is so emphatic when she talks about her boyfriend's erratic and chaotic life as she is so monotonous, dull, obsessive when she talks about her mother's temperament (which is her temperament when she identifies herself with the company). She does all this by raising rigid, hard boundaries, walls, among the various configurations of the Self.

The sessions too follow the same compartmentalized pattern: she describes her daily routine in detail, rigorously reviewing the various elements that characterize her day. She never brings in an affect, an emotion, a desire, a fantasy. When the patient's narrative or a sigh or a more prolonged silence opens a space, I intervene on the material, trying to bind it to some affective experience so as to stitch together all the seemingly disconnected elements that make up her Self.

Here is an excerpt from the session:

She goes on listing all the people to whom her mother does favours not to appear uninterested, while she had to go to the dentist for painful dental surgery and come back alone. Her mother did not offer to accompany her. *I'll take care of myself anyway*, she adds.

She seems crestfallen. I tell her that she looks despondent, maybe because of what she was telling. She adds:

> *I sleep on the couch and watch TV until late. Any mother would say, 'take this TV and stay in bed in your room'. But she doesn't. I get up in the morning and take a cold shower because the boiler is off. I told her and she said: 'take it in the evening when the heating is on'. But since she gets up in the morning and makes bread for grandma, why can't she turn the boiler on for me?*

She goes on to say that everything at home was targeted to her brother. Never a party, a moment, anything for her. Not even when she grew up. They could have shared some girly stuff just to feel like accomplices, but no. She even wanted her mother's reprimands when she came home late at night as a teenager; this would have shown that her mother had noticed her absence and instead nothing. She just did not exist and did not have to bother.

> *Life for my mother is like many little boxes that have to work and trouble if the sequence is disrupted; the rest doesn't exist. She never asked me: 'do you want this or that, do you like this or that?' She decides what has to be done and so she doesn't get anxious.*

I tell her that it was as if she had never felt her mother's pleasure of being with her, the pleasure of doing things with her. She answers:

> *Worse, it was as if I didn't even have to think or feel anything, no. It was as if I didn't exist. The less you exist, the better I am. That's her motto. So, she'd take me to the specialists, I'd shut up and they said I was stupid. So, she left me alone and didn't expect anything from me because even the specialists said I was stupid. She even told the teachers I was dumb. But she never helped me with my homework! Do you understand whom I live with?*

I say:

> *I understand your patience and pleasure in helping M's little niece with her homework. I understand your dedication when you play with M's young nieces and nephews and take care of all of them. Of course, in this way you make up for things you have never had and not worth looking for in your family ties! They somehow allow you to replenish with what you have not had and to feel adequate and adapted.*

She responds quickly, like an insight that has just arrived:

> *I no longer know what to say to my mother and even if tomorrow she wanted to get close to me again, what for? I found a pair of my jeans in the trash; I took them out and asked her for an explanation, she replied to me: they are old, enough, let's throw them away. I put them back. I decide when I no longer like something and throw it away.*

After this session, every time she leaves the room, she says that: *sooner or later, I will take one of your stuffed animals with me.*

Horizontal and vertical dimension

The closer we are to her Self, needy for care and attention, even regressed in her desire to have soft toys, the more rigid, inflexible, and intolerant she becomes at work. The striking element of her story is the unfolding of these two dimensions: the horizontal dimension of her existence, M's family like so many little siblings, and the vertical one, the maternal hierarchy, and the company. These two axes are not rearranged into a single 3D structure able to accommodate all these elements and transform them. Something is always missing. Even the language used in the story is different: in the horizontal dimension, it is fluid with an attuned prosody; in the vertical dimension, it is monotonous, with long monologues, interspersed with a few angry words, as if it came from somewhere else to interfere with her soliloquy. These angry interludes preoccupy the therapist because they seem to come from a split part that cannot be controlled and not accessible to dialogue.

Therefore, the psychotherapist has to support the patient's resources related to autonomy (which allow her to work and interact with her colleagues not in a too maladaptive way), and also to listen to all the aspects of the Self, from regressed and needy aspects to the hypercritical and paranoid ones.

It is clear that the patient redirects her transference onto structures and not onto objects, which leads to a greater temperamental rigidity and a lower emotional investment in objects. The analysis is not invested in the analyst's as a person (i.e. affects, relationship, interaction, need, and desire), but in its structural dimension: the setting and its precise space–time rules. The patient complies with all the rules of the setting, makes them her own, and proposes them back to the analyst, protesting when the analyst introduces a change (basically pauses linked to participation in conferences, holidays or midweek holidays). These changes (not arbitrary, but sometimes clearly linked to national holidays) are experienced by the patient as an abrupt disruption of continuity, which now seems to reside in the space–time structure of the setting.

During the summer holidays, she sleeps most of the time and almost never leaves her home, waiting to resume the sessions. This time discontinuation cancels the objects. Her mother, her boyfriend and his family, the holidays, the sea, do not exist in the absence of the space–time structure of the setting. It is as if, by taking the therapeutic setting away from her, I remove the skeleton holding her. During the following holidays, the patient does show up for her session. The psychotherapist understands the value of the patient's transference onto the structure and of being available at that moment accepts to see her anyway, given the importance of maintaining this scaffolding.

At the same time, the patient's choice to stay in the analytical room, even during a holiday, highlights her temperamental rigidity (and the strength of her defences) and an initial start of transference onto the object, i.e. also onto the analyst as a person and not only onto the structure of the setting. This new transference movement on the object allows the analyst to start broadening the analytical work to include softening the patient's defences (without fearing she may lose them suddenly and hence collapse); in fact, the transference onto the object paves the way to the deployment of affects in a less rigid way with respect to the transference onto the structure.

An extract from this period helps us better grasp this approach.

> *My mother does things the way she wants them, feels them, and it is her who decides, not the way EX needs them. Essentially, she gives you something when she decides. Now she'd like me to do more with her. But it's late. I'm sorry. She had to do it when I was younger, and I needed it.*

She speaks in a saddened tone (I feel her as small, fragile, and helpless); I suggest she seems to be saying there has always been a lot of dissonance between them (mum and EX); Both of them seem out of sync in time and space, without any harmony.

She answers with great sadness:

> *She said I was a difficult child; that I would stomp my feet; that I was stubborn. Maybe she didn't understand me; maybe she didn't know how to deal with me; or maybe she didn't consider me because only my brother was considered at home. I didn't exist; I was worthless, I didn't know how to do anything, I had no friends, I didn't know how to do my homework. Even now it's like that. She says I have lice because I don't wash. But when I needed her in the hospital, she wasn't there. Now it's late; it's useless for her to look for connectedness.*

Autobiography and bizarreness in dreaming

After two years of therapy, the patient can access her internal objects (but also concrete objects in a less persecutory manner) without the confusion, anxiety, and anger triggered by separation. She now shows a greater thought mobility, also represented through a dream (more than a year after the last dream brought in the session).

A passage from this period:

After having illustrated in detail what happened at work, after having specified what she did with M., after having listed all the things she did for her mum, and after having finished her usual tour of the various rooms, she remembers she had a dream. She is amazed because this had not happened to her for a long time; I can feel her joy in having a dream to tell, and I listen to her carefully.

> *I'm with my friend S. We're in the car, and she's driving. I'm sitting in the back. There are other people with me, but I don't remember who they are. Anyway, there are other people. We go, go, go; I don't know how we end up in Venice. We understand that we have gone a little too far from home and we have to go back. Along the highway, we meet three leprechauns that look like Santa Claus; they tell us some things; they are a bit crazy, one of them predicts that I will meet Mr Karl. I don't know who Mr Karl*

is, and I don't believe in their magic either. The fact is that it's as if they magically take us back to Rome, as if we are flying, because we immediately find ourselves in Rome and I know for sure that they did it.

The dream becomes an opportunity to access her autobiographical memories, fragmented and rearranged by her oneiric thought through which she traces back episodes and situations. Through this reconstruction, she finds again the chronological continuity of the events; she finds again the characters and places she knows. The bizarre element of the dream, the three leprechauns, is impossible to reconstruct. In wrapping up this chapter, it is crucial to stress that, beyond the contents of the dream, the dream function in the therapy features the characteristics described in the previous paragraph. A careful reading reveals all the elements of the dream: memory, intentionality and prediction, self-location and decontextualization, self-interaction, concerns, bizarre and irrational elements, hyperassociation, and much more.

The dream shows that many transformations have taken place, and that it is the right time to work more on defences. As illustrated in the previous paragraph, the patient's defences are so rigid that they create many problems for her, in her work, as well as in her interpersonal relationships. Currently, she shows more flexibility in moving her investment from one object to another, without becoming fragmented or without a strong dissociation. Since her transference onto the object is more stable (including the salvific vision of the three leprechauns, the three sessions, that predict her future and bring her magically back safe to Rome), it is possible to work on the rigidity of her defences to interrupt (or at least to transform) her transference onto the structure.

The third year of therapy: the silent transformations

She had an argument with some colleagues for being overzealous in calling the roll; the others did not defend her, and she changed rooms. She says that, by now, she is isolated. Nobody talks to her; they don't ask her for anything, they do the opposite of what she asks; if she goes into a room, they leave; they consider her stupid, a person who does not understand anything. (I note in my mind that this persecutory situation becomes worse in her working environment). And she goes on to tell what, in her opinion, they do against her, which she will report to her boss. She repeats the event several times with small pauses in her monologue, sighing; I do not understand what she says, when she sighs, because she uses a different tone of voice. During some longer pauses, I suggest she should link her persecutory thoughts to what happens in her workplace, and I ask her to give me her opinion. Her answer is always more or less similar. In short, she says, they hate her because she is dutiful, precise, consistent; she does what she is asked to do. If she does not have an assignment, she goes and asks to do the tasks of her colleagues; if she does not know what to do, she invents something; the other employees are all slackers, who are there doing nothing, waiting to be paid.

I propose to her a first food for thought, to which we may go back when and how she prefers.

I add:

First of all, sometimes you seem to speak to them on behalf of the company, as if it is the company speaking, and I wonder if they take it out on you, as you claim, because at that moment you represent the company and not EX. Second, the fact of representing the company, which is in your character, in your seriousness, in your sense of duty, may clash against those who don't like the company and therefore they seem to attack you, while they attack and spite the company, which you represent through your calls to order.

Through these two comments, we begin to emphasize some of the details of her requests (we break down her obsessiveness) that do not belong to 'EX', but to the company (separation from the identification with the company). The others cannot tolerate the situation, not because they cannot stand EX (reinforcement of identity), but because they have a different experience with the company (reinforcement of differences).

In this dialogue, she uses two different voices: the narrative voice that interacts with me, and the other one, almost sighing, that intercepts comments and criticism.

Anyway, this dialogue allows me to add something about her rigid stance (not very tolerant, inflexible, not very inclined to chatter, down to earth) that may lead her towards a new persecutory outbreak, since she resonates with the rigid response of the environment and her rigidity grows up to a breaking point. Moreover, in this company, whose style is far too soft and permissive, she runs the risk of being rejected because of her rigid and non-adaptive attitude.

In the here and now of the session, she does not seem to grasp in this comment the psychotherapist's concern about the persecutory stance that she is once again adopting in the company.

But, after the weekend break, a dream gives us new insights and shows the silent transformations taking place.

She tells me she had an incredible dream. She does not really know why she had it. Maybe the biological clock is calling. Here is the dream:

I'm about to give birth. It's Friday, and I know the baby is due on Saturday. My mum can't drive me because she's busy with Y (her partner); she tells me Z (my brother) will take me. That's all.

Her spontaneous associations are related not only to the Friday when EX remains without the analytical support, but to her mother, who is always there for everyone, always ready to help everyone else, except for her. And she lists the details of the things her mother does to meet the needs of others.

I try to put her in touch with her need (and therefore with her lack) for a 'mother-care agent-therapist' and with her pain for a mother-care agent-therapist who is not always available, but she intercepts my words as a concrete description of her mother and adds:

> *My mother is like that with me; she is different with the others; she is over caring. Doctor, my mother does not have a maternal instinct. Some women don't have it, and they shouldn't have children. She has no affection; she's not caring. I have so much affection to give; I like children, I don't know if I want to have any of my own.*

And she goes on to talk about her boyfriend's complex and numerous families.

I think she is not ready to work on her unmet needs, so I try to value the positive aspects of her dream, hinting at many things: she could give birth to something without anguish; she could give birth to something without her mother; she is able to schedule her delivery on Saturday without us.

She agrees and adds that she was calm and could manage everything by herself.

I capitalize on the strength of her comment and I go further, saying:

> *You give birth to something even without the help of your mother, who does not take care of you and entrusts you to your brother. A bit like what happened between us at the beginning, when your mother did not really know what to do with your breakdown and entrusted you to me. And we went our own way and reached the point in which you can deliver something of your own on Saturday.*

She agrees and tells me:

> *I can congratulate myself; I was good with the therapy without my mother ever getting directly into the session. It wasn't obvious that she wouldn't interfere. She dictates law everywhere, and then she doesn't care. Maybe that made me sick, too. She's tuned in to herself. She was also like that with Dad, and she continued to be like that when he left and we remained alone. As if nothing had happened. I still didn't exist. Now I can give birth to something new.*

Self knots

Despite many advances, she still has a rigid and inflexible basic structure, even if softer with respect to the past. This inflexible structure was determined by her primary bonds, the primary relational patterns through which she interacted with her caretaker.

The baby is immersed in these space–time patterns for a long time and absorbs their rhythm and characteristics. If these patterns are too rigid, binding, with almost zero degrees of freedom of movement, the resulting structure of the Self features indissoluble knots that bind it to a few movements. Untying these knots would lead to the fragmentation of the structure or to psychotic madness.

Pruning a tree with dry or diseased branches can revamp it to grow new branches; demolishing a building and preserving its basic components allows for reconstructing a new one; but such analogy cannot be used for the structure of the Self and psychotherapeutic treatment. Cutting off the dysfunctional branches of the Self, demolishing the basic elements of the building, would mean amputating large parts of the Self and disrupting its mental processes. In these cases, it is necessary to be patient and accompany the psychotic madness, providing it with new shoots (new grafts), making sure they come back to life, reshaping and strengthening the structure and gradually loosening old constraints to create new ones.

Sometimes the therapist has to untie the knots of the Self; sometimes, instead, he or she has to help the patient to tie them. A good therapy provides healing to the temporospatial fragmentation of the Self by tying the different threads and loose ends of time and space together. A good therapist does exactly that, often in an implicit way, by tapping into unchartered reservoirs of hidden and deeper meanings that are buried and encoded in the time and space dynamic. Those meanings may provide the glue to tie different lines of time and space and ultimately different biography lines together, and this glue is what leads to healing.

On the neuronal level, we assume that such glue is the brain's temporospatial dynamic which we discussed so extensively in this and in the previous chapters. So, a good psychotherapy may ultimately be a 'space–time therapy'.

References

Huang, Z., Obara, N., Davis, H.H., Pokorny, J., & Northoff, G. (2016). The temporal structure of resting-state brain activity in the medial prefrontal cortex predicts self-consciousness. *Neuropsychologia*, 82:161–170.

Wolff, A., Di Giovanni, D.A., Gómez-Pilar, J., Nakao, T, Huang, Z., Longtin, A., & Northoff, G. (2019). The temporal signature of self: Temporal measures of resting-state EEG predict self-consciousness. *Human Brain Mapping*, 40(3):789–803.

Chapter 7

Philosophical outlook
World, Time, and Self

World time is Self time

The evolution of the concept of the Self is somewhat similar to the theoretical vicissitudes of the multifaceted concept of time. Time went from being denied as a dimension (only a perceptual category) to an absolute dimension (Newtonian) at the end of the nineteenth century; since the beginning of the twentieth century, from Plank/Einstein onwards, it has become a subjective dimension. However, subjectivity of time is not tied to the individual person as distinct from the world. In contrast, the world itself is subjective rather than being purely objective, and time, that is, how the world constructs its own time, is essential for the intrinsically subjective nature of the world.

The Self has had the same fate; it has gone through and is still going through stages of total denial, i.e. the Self as a pure illusion, and of full structural recognition, i.e. the Self 'embedded' in the biology of the body. And the analogy goes even further. The Self constructs its own time as part of the ongoing construction of time in the world; the temporal features endow the Self with its subjectivity. If that construction of time is abnormal, the Self's subjectivity will change, as described in many case studies in this book. This will change the Self's trajectories within the environment; the Self can no longer steer its proper course in the world and its time. The world is time, time is the Self and, in this way, the Self becomes part of the world. This is the essence of our final Chapter. Let us look deeper into these concepts.

The passage of time

As pointed out by Rovelli (2018), Plato, in *Timeous*, provides a mathematical description of the shape of the atoms rather than of their motion. After Plato, many became fascinated with the analysis of shapes, with the description of things, and not with the analysis of events that unfold through time, i.e. of change. At first, Kepler too provided a mathematical description of orbits (shapes) as fixed objects, with no motion; therefore, he did not capture the dynamics of celestial bodies. Only by studying and describing these bodies,

DOI: 10.4324/9781003221876-8

was he able to see the events and changes taking place in the sky. Moreover, according to Rovelli (2018), the astronomy and physics from Ptolemy to Galileo, from Newton to Schrödinger, were related to the mathematical description of how things change, not how they are.

According to the French philosopher Jean-Marie Guyau (1890/1902), the time dilemma, also investigated by Aristotle, began with motion. If time does not have an absolute and hence a pre-existing structure but it emerges from the spatial relationships with the surrounding reality, then it can be seen as dependent on perceptual, subjective factors and so as belonging to the human mind. But let us take a step back.

The passage of time has fascinated the human mind for millennia. And it has been measured in many ways through sundials, hourglasses, mechanical, and digital clocks, or even, atomic clocks capable of capturing small instantaneous variations between two intervals. In any case, the most sophisticated way to measure time is surely our brain (Drayton & Furman, 2018). In fact, the brain can synchronously and quickly coordinate the sensory-motor response, synchronize the voice output, taking into account how time flows by reflecting on the past, on its unfolding, and by programming the future. Yet, there are no specific neuronal paths designed to process time per se. Time is in its structure or, as Rovelli says (Rovelli, 2017, 2018), time exists in us. The subjectivity of time is not only linked to how the brain measures time intervals and therefore to the estimated duration of an event or interval among several events, but, in a broader way, to the question of its nature.

St. Augustine placed time within the framework of '*distensio animi*';[1] Aristotle investigated this subject starting from the evidence that when time seems to flow, a movement occurs simultaneously (McKeon, 1941); but it was Newton (1713) who put forward its absolute nature and Kant (1781) it's *a priori* essence. Leibniz (Arthur, 1994) reviews the concept of time as independent of things; however, Berkeley (1710/2002) stated that time separated from ideas coming up in the spirit and considered as having an abstract duration is totally incomprehensible. In his treatise on human nature of 1738–1740, David Hume fiercely criticized Newton's absolute concept of time, bringing it back among the first impressions, among the perceptions of the real world, thus stripping it of its objectivity.

Space–time

Notwithstanding their strongly debated arguments on this subject, these philosophers and physicists laid the foundations of classical physics; it took until the twentieth century to go beyond the concept of absolute time and to bring it back to its complex relationship with space. In fact, last century was characterized by many changes; we would like to mention some of them.

Starting from Einstein in 1954, actually from Einstein's professor, Minkowski, space and time are no longer absolute, but relative with respect to the observer's reference system. Moreover, time does not have a uniform distribution and changes according to the space curvature. The absolute simultaneity between two events does not exist. Clocks never mark the same time either; time changes according to their movement and position in space. So, in the early 1900s, time became a variable linked to the observer, to the system, and the stage where events unfold is neither time nor space, but their 'space–time' union.

In the second half of the 1900s, DeWitt (1967), Wheeler & Weyl (1986) dealt a further death blow to the absolute concept of time, showing that time is not instrumental in describing the relationship between particles on a microscopic, quantum scale. This second revolution, after the first started by Einstein, led scientists to say that time does not exist outside of human existence. In the new millennium, this concept was instead reclaimed through the superstring theory (Gubser, 2010; Schwarz, 1998; t'Hooft, 2013), or more generally through the concept of entanglement (Gilder, 2008).

None of us can deny that time flows, that we are immersed in time and see it stretching between the past and the future, holding it anchored to the present. None of us dares to deny that this 'mental' time has a value other than the 'before and after' of physical time (Russell, 1915). In fact, due to the 'tensive' (Dorato, 1995; Dorato, 2013; McTaggart, 1908) directional value of mental time, none of us can imagine what a timeless reality is.

We all observe continuous changes pointing to the direction of time. How is it possible to reconcile this with the scientific postulates of the non-existence of time? One of the most plausible explanations of the existence or non-existence of time is the following: what is conspicuous for macrostructures has less value (fewer constraints) for microstructures (Rovelli, 2017); time disappears in the description of the interaction between particles or, more precisely, it is not necessary to describe their interaction. But in the transition from micro to macrostructures, it becomes an essential landmark to describe changes in the system. An equally interesting idea is that one part of the system acts as a clock for the others, and we perceive time because we are one of those pieces (Callender, 2010, 2017). Through Mott's experiment on the collision between a Helium nucleus and a larger one, Callender adds that:

> Remarkably, the atom, relative to the nucleus, obeys the standard time-dependent equation of quantum mechanics. A function of space plays the role of time. So even though the system as a whole is timeless, the individual pieces are not. Hidden in the timeless equation for the total system is a time for the subsystem [...] The universe may be timeless, but if you imagine breaking it into pieces, some of the pieces can serve as clocks for the others. Time emerges from timelessness. We perceive time because we are, by our very nature, one of those pieces.

> (Callender, 2010, p. 65)

He defines time as a great storyteller:

> In a very precise sense, time is the direction within space-time in which good prediction is possible—the direction in which we can tell the most informative stories. The narrative of the universe does not unfold in space. It unfolds in time.
>
> (Callender, 2010, p. 62)

The same holds true for the Self. The world unfolds in time, and the Self is part of the world; hence, the Self unfolds in the time of the world. That is literally true. Life events disrupt the flow of time in the world for the individual subject whose Self will consequently suffer from disruptions in its own construction of time. All the subject discussed in our case studies experienced an abnormal relationship of their Self to the world; we showed that this was driven by a deeper layer, the layer of the temporal relationship of the world and the Self.

Time is us

According to Rovelli (2018) and his description of the minimum form of time, time is not organized along a line (nor in Einstein's curved or smooth geometry), but it derives from the mutual interaction between 'quantums' (elementary grains) that are actualized in the moment they interact. It is their interaction that weaves the space–time canvas. Therefore, the 'time' variable is one of the many variables that describe the world. On our (meso/macroscopic) scale, we do not grasp its tiny (quantum) variations, and do not grasp the time discrepancies due to the speed of light; so, on our scale, we can think of time as determined. We can imagine it as a hard table with an extension called space and an entropic direction that we call time. Furthermore, if no variable of the system can play the role of 'time' in the domain of the theory of relativity, we may say that it is not the evolution over time that determines the state, but it is the state that determines time.

Translating this into our reference system, i.e. the Self, we may say that the Self does not record the flow of time as an (external and absolute) independent variable with respect to itself, but the Self is time, seen as its unfolding (possible) space–time configurations when parts interact. These (different time-related configurations) are recorded as time flows, or rather, these do represent our experience of time. Boltzmann understood this very well and talked about 'blurring', which leaves the world to its unpredictability, even if we can measure everything. Putting it simply, the variation of entropy in a system cannot be equal to zero, and so, it is the only equation that describes time in physics (Rovelli, 2017, 2018). The transition from low entropy systems to higher entropy systems describes the energy variations between systems (macroscopic state → energy → time), which are time variations. According to Rovelli (2017), if the past is a lower entropy system, it is possible to find traces of the past everywhere, but we will not find traces of the future.

The brain is full of traces of the past, as maps unfolding onto the present, but it has no similar maps for the future. The future can be decided, expected, predicted, but it leaves no traces. This is because the entropy of the past is lower than that of the present, which is lower than that of the future; it cannot be the other way around. The direction of the entropic variation does not allow us to change the past, but it does not prevent us from planning the future. All this, simplified to a narrative-linguistic version, creates our experience of time as uniform and directional. The before and after of time in physics are the past and the future of mental time. Our time arrow flies from birth to death, from the past to the present towards the future. It is a subjective perception determined by consciousness and the Self. So, what is the Self? It is exactly what we have described: a space–time extension, over-stratified in the memory traces that make up the maps, multi-determined by three elements (three place relations): internal elements, external elements, ranges of contexts (Ismael, 2007), the (immediate) external domain and the world. This interaction among these three elements is not homogeneous but has different degrees of freedom; it weaves the Self's fabric of relations, whose dynamism can be described at the microscopic (brain, neurons, synapses), and at the meso/macroscopic (person/system-environment) level. The Self's fabric of relations is ultimately nothing but the interweaving of the world time and the Self time; they are intimately coupled.

The dynamics of the Self

Rovelli (2018) warns us that we cannot draw a complete map of the events of the world; in fact, events, and among them the passage of time, only unfold through an interaction and with respect to a physical system involved in the interaction; no map can ever capture all the changes. A clearer descriptive example is the physics of the wheel touching the road on which it is moving always and only in one point. Neither the individual description of this contact point, nor that of the shape of the wheel, or the road, can account for the motion of the wheel (in space and time). This metaphor finds its limit in the linearity of the system considered; however, it helps to understand that, if we raise the question related to the nature of the Self within these linear limits, this question is as meaningless as the one on the nature of time.

In any case, let us go back to our description of the dynamics of the Self.

The Self does not have its own conformation; it is not an object, and it does not have an absolute structure that is independent of its relations with the three (internal/external/environmental) elements mentioned above; instead, it takes on spatial-temporal configurations ranging from minimal to more complex forms, as described in the various chapters. Not all configurations are possible, only those determined by the equilibrium that the system can reach at that moment. This local and unchanged punctiform (proper time, Eigenzeit) equilibrium marks the transformations of the system (the configurations of the Self), which appear to us as directional (time flow) for the traces (impressions, memories, somatic/psychic markers) left at the contact point of the three elements. The punctiform alignment of these traces is a map of the Self; it marks its discontinuity (contact point of the three elements) and its continuity (synchronic alignment). We have described this process as the dynamism of the Self. We can see it in detail through the analysis of spontaneous brain activity.

There is now strong evidence that the brain's spontaneous activity shows an elaborate spatiotemporal structure, in which, as Wolff et al. (2019) write:

> Faster frequencies are nested within the more powerful slower ones—this amounts to 'temporal nestedness'. Such temporal nestedness on the neuronal level may also be relevant on the psychological level of the self. As the self is preserved and manifested in both shorter and longer time scales, ranging from milliseconds over hours and weeks to years and decades, one would suspect 'temporal nestedness' to hold on the psychological level.
>
> (Wolff et al., 2019, p. 790)

There are many ways to measure the temporal structure of spontaneous activity, the authors consider:

> The autocorrelation window (ACW) (Honey et al., 2012; Murray et al., 2014). Simply put, the ACW measures the correlation in neural activity patterns across different points in a time series; the stronger the correlation between distant points in time, the longer the ACW. It thus indexes sameness or 'temporal continuity' of neural activity. It is still unclear how such 'temporal continuity' on the neuronal level is related to the self on the psychological level.
>
> (Wolff et al., 2019, p. 790)

The spontaneous brain activity also shows a strong capacity for cross frequency coupling (CFC) that may account for temporal integration.

Although there is no clear evidence on how to read the data on the brain's spontaneous activity and its correlations with the Self, the authors conclude that:

> Taken together, there is strong empirical evidence that (i) the brain's resting state activity—its spontaneous activity—is closely related to our sense of self, or self-consciousness (Davey et al., 2016; Northoff, 2016; Qin & Northoff, 2011); and that (ii) on a purely psychological level, the self can be characterized by strong temporal integration which includes temporal nestedness (manifest over different time scales or frequency ranges), temporal continuity (as in Self-continuity), and temporal integration.
>
> (Wolff et al., 2019, p. 790)

Temporal integration, temporal nestedness, temporal continuity, highlight the consistent work done by brain structures to account for our being located in the world; the Self is nothing more than the product of this continuous neuronal work. We are saying that the Self-span (Minkowski, 1933, spacelike-related) extends over different time intervals (Minkowski, 1933, timelike-related), which account for the continuity perceived on a psychological level as self-consciousness, and, for longer time spans, as the continuity of the Self and personal identity. We can say that a Longer ACW indicates that the neuronal activity remains the same over time and therefore accounts for Self-continuity.

Continuity and discontinuity, order and disorder, complexity

As widely described in psychoanalysis (by an impressive list of authors), the Self maintains the person-subjectivity connotation in this field, with very precise structural or relational characteristics. These features develop in early childhood through the interaction with the care-giver. Meissner (2008) captured their temporal value:

> What, then, do these considerations tell us about how we think about the Self in psychoanalysis? First, temporal experience of the self is not only tied to the body, but the temporality of the self *is* the temporality of the body—they are one and the same. The experience of myself as a body is captured in the same time frame as my experience of all material bodies in the world around me.
>
> (p. 726)

So, our history, our human existence, starts by introducing the body into the world. Our contact with the world is a slow enrichment of all our mental functions: it is like proceeding from some basic biological structure towards dreams, illusions, fantasies conveying an increasing complexity of the Self. This is a travel from the grounded Self to metaphorical language (metacognition, metastructure, and so on). That is to say, a gradual shift from the primitive form of embodiment, with more predictable structures in terms of behaviour (instinctive, sensory, and/or motor responses, primary reflexes), to broader configurations of the Self, extrinsically linked to the relationship with others, artistic production, the development of science, culture and social life. These configurations can be analyzed 'in hindsight' (*ex-post*), after they have left an imprint (memories) of the contact among the various elements from which they originated.

We could describe it with the language of physics, neuroscience, and psychoanalysis. The language used to describe a system adapts to the characteristics of the system; this adaptation is mediated through models. The psychoanalytic model is one of the many theories of the mind. When combined with modern research in the field of neuroscience and neuropsychology, it provides more information on how the mind works and its pathology. The extensive description of the clinical cases in the chapters of this book has allowed us to highlight this interconnection.

The description of the distortions or tears (discontinuities) of the Self, produced in the course of the existence by the laws of biology alone, does not account for the many variables of human experience: suffering, joy, pain, up to trauma and psychopathology. Similarly, we may ask ourselves if analysing all this through laws of hard sciences such as physics, can account for human experience.

By looking into the evolution of the concept of time in physics, we have understood that this language does not capture the essence of the human journey, from birth to death. The time span we call existence, with its directional arrow of time, but also with its unpredictable and irreversible actions, does not allow human existence to be easily framed in theoretical physics or in computational biology. The physics of complex non-linear systems has tried to go beyond the deterministic point of view, describing instability, non-equilibrium, irreversibility, chaos, and disorder as the fundamental keywords of a new science, also valid for living systems.

In the realm of physics of complex systems, the dynamic balance between continuity and discontinuity is called transformation. De Toni and Comello (2010) wrote: 'Searching for the dynamic equilibrium between continuity and discontinuity, i.e. transforming, means creating, adapting to and exploiting the vital coexistence between the two extremes' (p. 112).

Complex does not mean complicated, they add. What is complicated can be deployed in a linear way and analyzed in its single components. What is complicated can be disassembled and reassembled. Instead, complex means *cum plexum*, woven; it cannot be described with the analysis of the single parts that make up the system; it must be seen as a whole and described as synthesis; a single neuron does not describe the brain and the description of the brain does not describe the mind.

Bring back the Self to the world

A single element of the Self, among the many mentioned, does not make the 'Self'. The Self can be captured in synthesis, not in analysis. Therefore, they continue:

> The whole design cannot be understood by examining its single parts. Life cannot be reduced to an equation. Life can only be narrated. At the most, you can try and give a meaning to your life starting from your experience, ex post.
>
> (De Toni & Comello, 2010, p. 96)

Complex systems cannot be analyzed through their individual parts; complex systems can be narrated. For example, the references of the Self stored in memory pave the way to 'experience'; some of them retroactively seem to be nuclei of psychopathology, which act on the system, thus producing great changes that can be detected *ex-post* because the distortions of the Self have already worked (transformed) the whole system in the direction of psychopathology. Therefore, a single nucleus cannot be understood independently of the changes produced in the system.

From this point of view, we should correct what was described before in terms of relativity, determinism and quantum physics, in line with Prigogine's arguments, by quoting De Toni and Comello:

> Through the exchange of matter and energy with the external environment, open systems do not evolve towards a regular and irreversible increase in entropy (unlike closed systems, see second law of thermodynamics); on the contrary, they can evolve towards a state of bigger order. Hence, continuity and discontinuity, order and disorder, complexity [...] Which implies non-linearity and the unpredictable effects produced by small variations in the initial conditions.
>
> (De Toni & Comello, 2010, p. 23)

If the Self is part of the living human (complex adaptive systems, i.e. complex living systems with evolution abilities), we can define it through the elements that characterize living systems:

> As an unstable collection of elements and connections which are self-organized to ensure adaptation. Such a system is shaped consistently through time; it is adaptive and self-organized and is not managed or controlled by any single entity. The fundamental objective of adaptation is achieved through the regular redefinition of the relationship between the complex system and the external environment.
>
> (De Toni & Comello, 2010, p. 25)

Morin (2005, 2008) stressed that if a perfect order reigned in the universe, no new creation, and therefore no evolution would be possible; however, it would be equally impossible to live in pure disorder, since the ensuing instability would hamper any evolution. So, the balance in which life is possible is made up of continuity and discontinuity, breaks and changes, order and disorder, which follow one another, always creating new opportunities.

Is it possible to think that the analytical exchange is like this ongoing search for a new balance to give life to new configurations of the Self, not stiffened by pre- and post-hoc pathobiography constraints? In our opinion, the analytical exchange ultimately needs to re-balance the Self-based time and the world-based time, re-integrating and re-aligning the Self within the time of the world.

The psychoanalyst should work through timing; sometimes, it is not so important what the analyst says, its semantic meaning, but the timing of that very same semantics is. The semantic cognitive surface of the Self is grounded in a deeper dynamic layer of time, where the Self-based time intersects with the world-based time. Good therapy means to timely target such a deeper dynamic layer of the Self-based time in order to 'bring back the Self to the world'.

Note

1 For what we have said it is abundantly clear that neither the future nor the past exist, and … it is not strictly correct to say that there are three times, a present of past things, a present of present things and a present of future things. Some such different times do exist in the mind, but nowhere else that I can see. The present of past things is the memory, the present of present things is direct perception and the present of future things is expectation. If we can speak in these terms I can see three times and I admit that they do exist. Augustine Saint. [Book XI, section 20, p. 26]. R. S. Pine-Coffin, 2002 (Augustine, 2002).

References

Arthur, R. (1994). Space and relativity in Newton and Leibniz. *British Journal for the Philosophy of Science*, 45 (1): 219–240.

Augustine (Saint). (2002). *The confessions* (R. S. Pine-Coffin, Trans.). New York: Penguin Books.

Berkeley, G. (1710/2002). *A treatise concerning the principles of human knowledge*. Dublin: Pepyat.

Callender, G. (2010). Is time an illusion? *Scientific American*, 6:59–65.

Callender, G. (2017). *What makes time special?* Oxford: Oxford University Press.

Davey, C. G., Pujol, J., & Harrison, B. J. (2016). Mapping the self in the brain's default mode network. *NeuroImage*, 132:390–397.

De Toni, A. F., & Comello, L. (2010). Journey into complexity. Lulu ebook, *Viaggio nella complessità*. Venezia: Marsilio Editori.

DeWitt, B.S. (1967). Quantum theory of gravity. The canonical theory. *Physical Review*, 160: 1113–1148.

Dorato, M. (1995). Ontological determinateness in quantum mechanics and special relativity. In C. Garola & A. Rossi (Eds.), *The foundations of quantum mechanics*. Dordrecht: Kluwer.

Dorato, M. (2013). *Che cos'è il tempo? Einstein, Goedel e l'esperienza comune*. Roma: Carocci Editore.

Drayton, L. & Furman, M. (2018). Thy mind, thy brain and time. *Trends in Neurosciences*, 41(10):641–643.

Einstein, A. (1954). *Relativity: The special and general theory*. Fifth Ed. London: Methuen.

Gilder, L. (2008). *The age of entanglement: when quantum physics was reborn*. New York: Alfred A. Knopf.

Gubser, S.S. (2010). *The Little Book of String Theory*. Princeton: Princeton University Press.

Guyau, J. M. (1890/1902). *La Genèse de l'Idée du Temps*. Second Ed. Paris: Alcan.

Honey, C. J., Thesen, T., Donner, T. H., Silbert, L. J., Carlson, C. E., Devinsky, O., Hasson, U. (2012). Slow cortical dynamics and the accumulation of information over long timescales. *Neuron*, 76:423–434.

Hume, D. (1738/1740). *A treatise of human nature: A critical edition*. Oxford: Oxford University Press, 2007.

Ismael, J.T. (2007). *The situated self*. Oxford: Oxford University Press.

Kant, I. (1781). *Critique of pure reason*. (P. Guyer & A.W. Wood Trans & Ed). Cambridge: Cambridge University Press. 1998.

McKeon, R. (1941). *Basic works of Aristotle*. New York: Random House.

McTaggart, J. (1908). The unreality of time. *Mind*, 18:457–484.

Meissner, W.W. (2008). Self and time. *Journal of The American Academy of Psychoanalysis and Dynamic Psychiatry*, 36(4):707–736.

Minkowski, E. (1933). *Lived time: Phenomenological and pathological studies*. Evanston: Northwestern University Press.

Morin, E. (2005). *Restrained complexity, generalized complexity*. Presented at the Colloquium 'Intelligence de la complexité: Epistémologie et pragmatique', Cerisy-La-Salle, France, June 26.

Morin, E. (2008). *On complexity*. New York: Hampton Press.

Murray, J. D., Bernacchia, A., Freedman, D. J., Romo, R., Wallis, J. D., Cai, X., Wang, X.-J. J. (2014). A hierarchy of intrinsic timescales across primate cortex. *Nature Neuroscience*, 17: 1661–1663.

Newton, I. (1713). *Philosophiae naturalis principia mathematica*. Cambridge: Crownfield.

Northoff, G. (2016). Is the self a higher-order or fundamental function of the brain? The "basis model of self-specificity" and its encoding by the brain's spontaneous activity. *Cognitive Neuroscience*, 7:203–222.

Qin, P., & Northoff, G. (2011). How is our self related to midline regions and the default-mode network? *NeuroImage*, 57:1221–1233.

Rovelli, C. (2017). Is time's arrow perspectival? In K. Chamcham, J., Silk, J. D., Barrow, & S. Saunders (Eds), *The philosophy of cosmology*. Cambridge: Cambridge University Press.

Rovelli, C. (2018). *The order of time*. New York: Riverhead Books.

Russell, B. (1915). On the Experience of Time. *Monist*, 25:212–233.

Schwarz, J. H. (1998). Recent developments in superstring theory. *Proceeding of the National Academy Science U S A*, 95(6):2750–2757.

t'Hooft, G. (2013). On the foundations of superstring theory. *Foundations Physics*, 43:46–53.

Wheeler, J.A., & Weyl, H. (1986). The unity of knowledge. *American Scientist*, 74:366–375.

Wolff, A., Di Giovanni, D.A., Gómez-Pilar, J., Nakao, T., Huang, Z., Longtin, A., & Northoff, G. (2019). The temporal signature of self: Temporal measures of resting-state EEG predict self-consciousness. *Human Brain Mapping*, 40(3):789–803.

Index

Page numbers followed by 'n' refer to notes.